*". . . consider to whom did it first occur to
include in a little ball all the sorts of flowers
which clothe the meadows in spring."*

Marc Antonio Sabellico
*De Situ Urbis Venetae,* Book III, 1490's

# Paperweights:
# "Flowers which clothe the meadows"

Paul Hollister
Dwight P. Lanmon

The Corning Museum of Glass
Corning, New York 14830

A special exhibition
The Corning Museum of Glass
Corning, New York

April 29—October 21, 1978

This project is supported by a grant from the National Endowment
for the Arts in Washington, D.C., a Federal Agency.

Printed in U.S.A.
Standard Book Number 0-87290-065-7
Library of Congress Catalog Card Number 77-91357

Design: Anthony Russell /Amanda Lester
Photography: Raymond F. Errett and Nicholas L. Williams
Production: David Towasser

"I hold every man a debtor to his profession; from the
which as men of course do seek to receive countenance and profit,
so ought they of duty to endeavour themselves by way of
amends to be a help and ornament thereunto."

(Francis Bacon 1561-1626)

The Honorable Amory Houghton is a man whose family history and professional life have been synonymous with glass. As President, Chairman, and now Chairman Emeritus of Corning Glass Works, he has presided over the formation of the Dow Corning Corporation, Owens-Corning Fiberglas Corporation, Pittsburgh Corning Corporation, and a one hundred and sixty fold increase in the size of his own company.

Among the ornaments brought to his vocation during this tenure were the rebirth of Steuben Glass in its unique quest for excellence; the Corning Glass Center and The Corning Museum of Glass, dedicated to the art, history, and science of all glass everywhere; and the Corning Glass Works Foundation, devoted to the improvement of the human environment and to intellectual and cultural growth. It was he who personally initiated a museum endowment fund for the acquisition of major pieces of glass; with his help a dramatic new Museum to house, protect, and utilize our vast collections will soon be constructed. Major among its treasures will be the superb paperweights acquired with great knowledge and taste over almost half a century by Ambassador Houghton.

Here is a man from the glass industry who may well have had more impact on it worldwide than any man of this century, a man who knows and loves the best in that most intricate of glass arts. To him this exhibition and catalogue are respectfully dedicated.

Thomas S. Buechner, Director
The Corning Museum of Glass

As nineteenth-century glassmakers explored the possibilities resulting from a headlong technological race, a number of new and dramatically different types of glass were developed. In a period when extravagance of design was often regarded as a positive attribute, French paperweights provide a respite of exquisite craftsmanship and conservative artistry. They may have been only colorful "baubles" when they were new, but today they are remarkable for their purity of material and perfection of execution, appreciated and prized for the charm of their design and the daring of their color combinations. Their peak was short-lived but brilliant, and their progeny are myriad on both sides of the Atlantic.

To celebrate these artistic and technical achievements in glassmaking, this catalogue (and the exhibition it accompanies) illustrates in color and full size some 300 of the most extraordinary paperweights that can be found today. They were selected from the total range of nineteenth-century American and European weights. There was no attempt to make the exhibition a lexicon of types; rather, the examples were chosen for their quality of design and execution — rarity alone was not a criterion. Several apparently unique specimens have been included, but so have weights which collectors might call "common." Some well-known types are missing in the following pages; others are shown in several refreshing variations. We have attempted to collect the majority of known examples of only one type: those weights which enclose realistic salamanders and flowering plants. They are thought by many to be the greatest technological achievements of the paperweight makers, and the group has never been assembled in one place in recent times.

The inherent pleasures of preparing an exhibition and catalogue of such beautiful objects were augmented by the enthusiasm of all of the individuals — collectors, dealers, museum professionals, and manufacturers — with whom we came in contact. To acknowledge their assistance is the most agreeable of duties:

First, and most importantly, to the Hon. Amory Houghton. In his own collection he demonstrated the wisdom of searching for only the highest quality and conceived the guidelines of this exhibition.

To Paul Hollister. His aesthetic discrimination helped transform those guidelines into reality, and his willingness to provide the lucid introduction which follows makes this catalogue infinitely more important.

For continual encouragement and enthusiasm, we owe a special debt of gratitude to Mr. and Mrs. Paul Jokelson.

Forty-two lenders unhesitatingly opened their cabinets to us; without their generosity, there would be no exhibition. To those named below, and to those who wish to remain anonymous, we tender our special thanks:

The Art Institute of Chicago (Mr. John Keefe); Baccarat, Inc.; Municipality of Baccarat (Mr. André Vulliet); Batiste (London); The John Nelson Bergstrom Art Center and Museum (Mrs. Jack W. Casper); G. E. Carter; Compagnie des Cristalleries de Saint-Louis (Mr. Gèrard Ingold and Mr. Claude Loisel); Mary Rich De Waters; Mr. and Mrs. Regnault Fairchild; Mr. Nelson Gustin; Heritage Plantation of Sandwich (Mr. and Mrs. Ladd MacMillan); the Hon. and Mrs. Amory Houghton; Illinois State Museum (Miss Betty L. Madden); Mr. Roger Imbert and Miss Caroline Imbert; Mr. and Mrs. Gèrard Ingold; Mr. and Mrs. Paul Jokelson; Dr. and Mrs. Junius T. Langston; Mr. Louis Lyons; Emma Gillinder Masland; Mr. and Mrs. Bernard Moos, Jr.; Musée du Conservatoire National des Arts et Métiers; The New-York Historical Society (Miss Mary Black); Old Sturbridge Village (Mr. Henry J. Harlow); Mr. Arthur Rubloff; Mr. and Mrs. Franklin Schuell; Spink & Son, Ltd. (Miss Pat McCawley and Mr. David Spink); Mr. and Mrs. Alan E. Symonds; Alan Tillman (Antiques), Ltd. (Mr. and Mrs. Alan Tillman, Miss Virginia Young); Dr. and Mrs. Daniel S. Turner; and fourteen others.

Others assisted us in the various and complex arrangements for photography, cataloguing, receiving, etc.; their help was vital: Mr. Brand Inglis, London; at Steuben Glass in New York, Miss Mary Minstrell and Miss Mary McHugh; the Art Institute of Chicago, Robert C. Carter and Richard Whitaker; the entire staff of The Corning Museum of Glass, and especially Adrian Baer, Gail Bardhan, Charleen Edwards, Ray Errett, Greg Farmer, Norma Jenkins, Jane Lanahan, Priscilla Price, Antony Snow, Nick Williams, and Virginia Wright.

Polly Guth and Monette Booth helped to establish order in every area, from cataloguing to installation.

Finally, there remains the acknowledgement of one very special person for his unflagging interest and cheer. Without the enduring and scholarly interest in the subject, the thoughtful counsel, always freely given, and the unselfish personal assistance of Mr. Tim Clarke, this exhibition would not be.

Dwight P. Lanmon
*Deputy Director, Collections*
*The Corning Museum of Glass*

## PAPERWEIGHT PRODUCTION

Glass paperweights first appeared in Europe in the mid-1840's. They were displayed at industrial exhibitions in Vienna (1845), London (1848), and elsewhere and could be purchased cheaply in stationers' and "fancy" shops which carried them in quantity. For want of more precise limits the decade 1845-1855 is now recognized as the "classic" period of paperweight making in Europe, especially in France, where the greatest number of weights and the finest were produced. The year 1845 is the earliest known date inside any paperweight (from Murano, Italy, and from the factory of Saint-Louis in France), or outside on the gilt metal mount of a pedestal weight from the Clichy factory (see p. 43, No. 100). The arbitrary closing date of 1855 is intended merely to indicate a time after which there is little in contemporary literature or exhibition catalogues to indicate continuing production of paperweights in Europe and Great Britain. Nevertheless, a number of paperweights from the Baccarat factory were made in 1858 to commemorate a visit of Maréchal Canrobert to Baccarat (p. 27, No. 10) and, from time to time, weights were engraved on the surface with initials and later, dates, indicating private occasions (p. 119, No. 238).

In England, the beginning of the classic period can be marked by the 1848 date which appears in many paperweights and inkwells from the Whitefriars factory of London. Undated paperweights from the Bacchus factory of Birmingham are listed in exhibitions in 1848 and 1849, joined in the latter year by weights from the Islington factory, also of Birmingham. These were said to have been produced to rival Bohemian paperweights that had been flooding the English market.

The first world's fair, the Great Exhibition of 1851 in London's Crystal Palace, with its large American section and many American visitors, provided the bridge by which foreign paperweights, and with them the paperweight craze, reached American shores. American paperweight making begins in 1852 with dated weights made by the New England Glass Company. Horace Greeley mentions the display of paperweights from Murano, Italy, and from the French factory of Clichy at the New York Crystal Palace exhibition of 1853. In America the classic period of paperweight making extends through the late 1870's, long after their popularity had apparently declined in Europe.

In France a small but important paperweight revival would seem to have coincided with the Paris Universal Exposition of 1878, where three-dimensional flora and fauna subjects are attributed without proof to the Pantin factory. It has been suggested that sporadic production occurred at Baccarat around 1900.

## THE TECHNICAL HERITAGE

The term, classic, used to specify European and American glass paperweights of the mid-nineteenth century, refers both to the perfection of the techniques used to produce the brilliantly colored yet reserved internal designs and to the full use of the magnifying dome of glass. Classic paperweight designs were produced by two ancient techniques: drawn glass canes with internal designs and drawn and twisted glass canes with threadlike twists; and also, by lampwork, a technique dating from the late sixteenth century; and by incrustation, an eighteenth-century technique. The first two of these techniques are almost as old as glassmaking itself.

The first technique, by which a solid glass rod with a design running lengthwise through it from end to end is produced, is now called millefiori. However simple or complex the design and the varying techniques of its execution, the cane is nearly always stretched or drawn out while hot (plastic) to reduce the diameter of its design. Miniaturization of the design doubtless has the effect of eliminating any defect or secret of construction that could otherwise be seen with the naked eye, but at the same time it creates a tiny image that is enchanting, whether it be a human portrait head, an animal silhouette, or a flower. When it has cooled, the cane—now long and pencil thin—can be cut in cross-section, creating a large number of slices that repeat the continuous design. Drawn canes with miniaturized motifs appeared in vessels from Mesopotamia as early as the fifteenth century B.C.

In the third century B.C. Hellenistic portrait head canes of extraordinary detail were being produced. Mold-blown bowls are ornamented with drawn canes, and some are made entirely of drawn and twisted canes laid parallel. These drawn and twisted canes, today called filigree, were made by the second of the ancient techniques and were used centuries later in glass paperweights. In filigree, as in millefiori cane making, the threaded design ran lengthwise, but on the outside of the cane. As it was drawn out, the cane was twisted to produce a rope-like spiraled design about the cylindrical surface of the cane.

In Rome and the Roman-dominated Near East of 100 B.C. to 100 A.D., production of molded bowls with rope-twist rims and allover millefiori designs of slices from drawn canes was greatly increased. These lovely bowls, the glory of Roman glassmaking, were praised by contemporary writers and maintained their reputation even though buried during the succeeding centuries. The Roman term for these wares is not known. So far as I have been able to determine, the apt term, *millefiori,* derived from the Italian words for *thousand* and *flowers*, was coined to describe the effect of this sort of overall cane decoration only in 1836, and then by a German, Heinrich von Minutoli. The word has stuck and will be used here because it is now part of the language of glass and is vital in describing classic period glass paperweights.

In Kenchreai, Greece, late fourth-century A.D. mosaic panels of fitted, shaped plaques, many made by the millefiori technique, have recently been discovered. Sumptuous Celtic jewelry found in Ireland, seventh- to ninth-century millefiori-decorated objects found at Jarrow, England, and ninth-century wall plaques and millefiori vessels from Samarra, north of Baghdad, Iraq, may be only the first elements of a grand historical continuity in which millefiori glass in one form or another was produced from place to place and century to century.

We pick up the trail of millefiori with the open-ended observation made about 1494 by the Venetian librarian-historian, Sabellico, who, writing on the glass industry on the Venetian island of Murano, said, " . . .age vero cui pri[m]o venit i[n] me[n]te[m] brevi pila i[n]cludere o[mn]ia floru[m] genera q[ui]bus verna[n]tia vestiunt[ur] prata. . . ." ("But, consider to whom did it first occur to include in a little ball all the sorts of flowers which clothe the meadows in spring. . . ."). Sabellico was probably referring to small, solid glass spheres in which a gather of clear glass has been covered with an outer layer of glass containing a random assortment of slices from chevron-design millefiori canes. One of these spheres was illustrated by Apsley Pellatt in his *Curiosities of Glass-Making* (1849), and a number of others have recently been located in European museums. Some are solid, showing the pontil mark where the glass was held during fabrication on the pontil rod; others have been drilled through to be mounted as decorative objects or suspended from chains. One elaborately mounted, hollow example in

Veste Coburg has been blown. A Venice-Murano origin seems certain for most of them (p. 26, No. 1)

Blown Venetian vessels such as chalices or cups, bottles, and small ewers show flattened chevron canes similar, often identical, to those found in the millefiori spheres and are datable by their style to the closing years of the fifteenth and early sixteenth centuries. In a somewhat later context, T. H. Clarke has raised the possibility that the "two little standing Cuppes with covers chalice fashion of glass of many colours" from Henry VIII's inventory of 1542 are the two lovely blown millefiori ewers in The British Museum. Recent research by Luigi Zecchin has brought to light further evidence of late fifteenth-century millefiori production: an inventory of the Giovanni Barovier factory made in 1496 in which glass dagger handles and other objects containing "rosettes" are listed. The likelihood is proposed by Zecchin that Barovier's sister Rosa operated a workshop in which colored canes were produced to be made into millefiori "rosettes." Edward Dillon says that the contemporary term for chevron bead was *perle à rosette*.

Slightly later, presumably at the same time that blown filigree glass vessels were introduced in Venice in the mid-sixteenth century, lengths of filigree were combined with millefiori in glass spheres. Filigree glass of great variety and complexity continued to be produced in Venice through the seventeenth century, by which time it was closely imitated in the Netherlands, Germany, and elsewhere. During the seventeenth and eighteenth centuries millefiori cane slices and lengths of filigree appeared together in such small luxury items as the glass handles of steel-bladed knives. In 1709 King Frederick IV of Denmark, returning from a trip to Venice, brought back a large collection of the popularly elaborate Venetian glass, including purely ornamental knives, forks, and spoons made entirely of filigree glass, which may now be seen in the royal pleasure seat of Rosenborg Castle in Copenhagen. Millefiori and filigree also appeared together with lengths of opaque white and colored ribbon in glass columns, wrapped about a copper core, which were perhaps intended as finials or as architectural elements in curio cabinets or chandeliers of the eighteenth century. One such column in the Hollingworth Magniac sale of 1892 at Christie's measured 15¾ inches in length and another presently in The British Museum is two inches longer.

The third paperweight technique derived from the past, though not as ancient as the millefiori and filigree cane techniques, is lampwork: glass either blown or manipulated from clear or colored glass rods over a torch or blow-lamp. Glass is thought to have been lampworked in Venice at the end of the sixteenth century, in Nevers, France, and elsewhere in Europe during the seventeenth and eighteenth centuries. Exquisitely detailed scenes framed in shadow boxes containing tiny glass figures, trees, flowers, running brooks, even realistic miniature ferns rival, if not surpass, any lampwork seen in the nineteenth-century paperweights.

The fourth process used in the nineteenth century in the making of glass paperweights involved the insertion or "incrustation" into glass of foreign, non-glassy matter. The technique was probably introduced during the last third of the eighteenth century in Scotland, England, and Bohemia in response to the various neo-classicisms popular in Europe at that time. They were then called cameo incrustations, or *crystalloceramie*; today they are known as sulphides. These molded cameo portraits and designs, of a secret formula—most likely a silica-clay paste—were inserted into a variety of glass objects in addition to paperweights, notably pendants, scent bottles, tumblers, decanters, jewel boxes, knife rests, vases, plates, pitchers, candlesticks, and religious ornaments. As the popularity of these wares increased, methods of incrustation were patented by Saint-Amans in 1818 in France, closely followed by Apsley Pellatt in 1819 in England. Pellatt's method enclosed the cameo in a glass envelope, which was then deflated to seal it, and applied like a wafer to the surface of the object it was intended to enhance. The earliest molded cameos retained the circular outline of the medals from which the subjects were usually taken; but in paperweights of the 1840's sulphide subjects frequently had intricately detailed outlines such as one sees in the Baccarat "Huntsman and Dog" and "Joan of Arc" sulphide paperweights (p. 117, Nos. 84, 85), which were probably made by a die process similar to that used to produce Wedgwood's jasper cameo wares. Paperweights were also incrusted with painted sulphides and with gold foil enameled to show famous Napoleonic and other medals, coats of arms, flowers, and portraits. Altogether, however, incrustation accounts for only a fraction of the weights produced in the classic period of paperweight making.

THE CLIMATE OF REVIVAL, 1750-1845

Curiosity about elaborately or exquisitely made objects, especially objects of antiquity, was the eighteenth-century collector's obsession. Almanacs and books on antiquities were published which listed the addresses and specialties of collectors, dealers, and connoisseurs. The "curio" cabinets of the collectors filled with "curiosities," objects of unknown origin but great interest. "I am especially pleased with a little ball of pale yellow glass," writes the Abbé Barthélemy to the Comte de Caylus in 1756, "with clusters of white enamel ranged perpendicularly around the circumference." This may have been one of the Renaissance-period spheres referred to above, as the matrix glass was often a pale yellow.

Caylus and Barthélemy corresponded over the discoveries near mid-century of Herculaneum and Pompeii, and in 1756 Caylus embarked on his seven-volume *Recollections of Antiquity*, in which he described the mosaic-millefiori process with surprising insight and plausibility. Caylus also mentions a brisk trade in *copies* of ancient glass being sold as ancient. The posthumous publication of Winckelmann's *Art of The Ancients* (1776) claimed that ancient glass fragments were being remelted.

The revival of the millefiori technique perhaps begins in 1786 with the experiments of a German named Brückmann. By the early 1800's the excavations in and around Rome stimulated interest in every sort of ancient glass. The Dodwell Collection, formed from about 1806 to 1832 and now in the Staatliche Antikensammlungen und Glyptothek Museum, Munich, included freely interpreted imitations of Roman bowls, perhaps inspired by examples then being excavated from Etruscan tombs north of Rome. W. E. Fuss is known to have succeeded in making millefiori in Silesia in 1833; in 1837 Friedrich Egermann's glass formulas giving mosaic and millefiori color combinations were found at the Zenker works in Bohemia. Small millefiori bottles, ornaments, buttons, and jewelry items were produced in and around Gablonz (now Jablonec nad Nisou) in northern Bohemia. In 1842 Fuss exhibited his millefiori in Mainz, and millefiori production was carried on for the next decade in the Silesian workshop of Franz Pohl.

Meanwhile, by 1839 the great French glassmaker, Georges Bontemps, had succeeded in producing filigree glass, a process the details of which he was to reveal in 1845 in a widely acclaimed treatise that has since become the bible of filigree making. By 1844 Bontemps had also produced millefiori, but apparently confined himself to the reproduction of ancient millefiori fragments and produced no paperweights.

THE CLASSIC PERIOD OF PAPERWEIGHT MAKING, 1845-1855

After 1800 the impetus given the decorative arts by an expanding industrial technology led to European national exhibitions of ever-greater size and scope, particularly in France. In terms of millefiori and lampwork production, the increased use of writing paper and the accessories and regalia of letter writing, as well as that of toiletry and perfumery were direct stimulants to decorative novelties. In addition to paperweights, millefiori inkwells, wafer dishes for wax letter seals, penholders (called shotcups), filigree straightedges, and the trays to hold them all, there were scent bottles, dresser sets with lampworked paperweight stoppers, candy boxes, millefiori goblets and wine glasses, flower vases with filigree bowls and paperweight bases, mantel ornaments, wig stands, and other novelties both useful and purely decorative.

But glass paperweights were produced in by far the greatest quantity and variety because they were cheap to make and to buy, small and easy to carry home as gifts or as souvenirs to put on the desk, the étagère, or the "whatnot." For perhaps a decade the quality crystal glass factories of the Continent and, to a lesser extent, of England carried them as part of their regular production.

Although someone in Venice-Murano could well have produced the paperweights at any time after the fifteenth century simply by grinding flat the pontil area of a Venetian ball, they are first noted in 1845. Because of the comments of Professor Eugène Péligot of the Conservatoire des Arts et Métiers, Paris, following his visit made at the behest of the Paris Chamber of Commerce to the Exhibition of Austrian Industry held in Vienna in 1845, where he saw the paperweights of Pietro Bigaglia, Venice has come to be credited with making the first paperweights. The implication has been that, on his return to Paris, Péligot informed the Saint-Louis factory, who immediately began producing paperweights dated 1845. On the contrary, the chronology of millefiori making presented in this introduction should have demonstrated not only the considerable time and experimentation required to produce millefiori but also the simultaneity of experimentation in different parts of Europe from the 1830's on.

Interestingly enough, there is little apparent development in the Venetian fashion of paperweight making. Even Venetian paperweights bearing dates as late as 1847 and 1849 are not paperweights in the classic period sense. As defined here, the "classic" paperweight is characterized by an orderly interior millefiori or lampworked design set low, near the base of the weight, and covered by a magnifying dome of clear glass, usually a lead glass. The base of the weight is ground out to remove the pontil mark, leaving a slight concavity that is often decorated with a cut star. If the base is ground flat it is decorated with strawberry cutting or cross-hatching. The brilliant glass of the dome above the design is often faceted with flat or concave cuts, and overlaid or cased with one or more colors, which in turn are sometimes even gilded.

In Venetian weights the scrambled design nearly fills the weight, coming close to the surface of a dome of usually bubbly, tinted glass that neither magnifies nor enhances the random interior design. The base is ground flat and thus is easily scratched, but scratches make no difference since one cannot see through to the base of the weight.

By contrast, French paperweights from the Saint-Louis factory bearing the same "earliest" date of 1845 show a sophistication of techniques that must have required several years to achieve. Though a few of the close-packed millefiori designs are still set near the dome of the weight, complicated mushroom designs with filigree *torsades* dated 1845 already have the clear, carefully shaped dome that magnifies the design. By 1846 Baccarat has achieved virtually the same result. The same is true also of Bohemian lime-potash glass paperweights, though none has yet turned up with a date earlier than 1848, and the glass is not as clear as the French lead glass.

From 1846 the classic paperweight profile is established of a low-set design under a clear, magnifying dome. This paperweight form traveled from the Continent to England and thence to the United States, where it remained virtually unchanged through the 1870's. The classic paperweight proved to be an ideal glass form: natural to glassmaking because round, desirable because small, mysterious because of its miniature designs under a magnifying dome, brilliant to the eye, cool and good to hold in the palm of the hand.

It became obvious to the famous Old French crystal glass factories of Baccarat (founded 1764 in Alsace) and Saint-Louis (1767 in Lorraine) that in paperweights they had a saleable novelty item, something strikingly different from the cloudy opaline and cut and molded crystal they had been making for over a decade. They began adding new paperweight designs to their line, which included for each factory at least a dozen different types of millefiori and lampworked designs, each type with numerous variations and color combinations. They were in competition, but together they had long enjoyed a near monopoly on luxury glass in France. Along with the Choisy-le-Roi factory of Georges Bontemps and one or two other factories they even shared the same distributor, Launay Hautin & Co., of Paris, then the center of the cultured world. But at the Paris Exposition of 1844 Baccarat and Saint-Louis were challenged by the arrival on the fine crystal scene of Clichy, a factory set up by Maës and Clémendot in what was then a suburb of Paris. By 1845 Clichy added paperweights to its line of overlaid glass in the universally popular Bohemian style. The struggle for paperweight supremacy was on.

This spirited competition carried right through the financially critical and politically bloody years surrounding the Revolution of 1848, and while Choisy-le-Roi and other factories went out of business, the big three—now including Clichy—continued to produce paperweights in quantity and variety. The fierceness of the competition is revealed in broad strokes in the correspondence (1847-1851) of the distributor Launay to the director of Saint-Louis, berating the factory for making poor paperweights, specifying how they should be improved, and complaining that the market was being lost to Clichy. In 1849 Baccarat exhibited a broad sampling of its weights at the big Paris Exposition—the largest French national exhibition ever held—and a similar selection at the Paris (international) Exposition of 1855. Prices given for the weights exhibited were extremely reasonable, the snakes so highly valued today being priced at only ten francs. Color sketches in the Baccarat archives give exact dimensions for each lampworked flower and for the corresponding diameter of the enclosing dome. Paperweights were a precise and vigorous production item in which the same designs were repeated with only the slight variations inherent in individual craftsmanship.

In the matter of paperweights at least, as indicated in the Launay correspondence, Clichy indeed appears to have outmaneuvered its two rivals and to have enjoyed critical acclaim. Clichy was the only one of the three French factories to have exhibited at the Crystal Palace, London, in 1851. There it received the Council Medal for its new "boracic" optical glass introduced two years earlier. This soda-based, zinc oxide glass, in which boric acid was used as a flux, was said to be free from bubbles, striae (streaks), and foreign matter. (It is not presently known if this lighter glass was used in paperweights, but as late as the Paris Universal Exhibition of 1867 Clichy was complimented on its exhibit of fine *flint*, presumably lead, glass.) Reporting on glass for the French Commission to the Great Exhibition of 1851, Eugène Péligot (who had reported on Bigaglia's Murano weights in Vienna in 1845) noted the admirable quality of Clichy's "rose overlays recalling the Du Barry pink of old Sèvres china, and flawless turquoise blue, muslin, filigree, and millefiori glass in the most varied designs."

Three Clichy millefiori pieces have been reasonably documented as having been exhibited at the Great Exhibition. One is a large spaced millefiori design engraved on the base with a crown above the VA monogram (for Queen Victoria and Prince Albert) and the notation "Londres [London]/1851." A Clichy sulphide of Victoria on a purple-black ground, bearing a sticker that read, "Exhibition, Hyde Park, London 1851," was offered at auction a few years ago. The third, a millefiori scent bottle with stopper, was shown in *The Illustrated Exhibitor*, a contemporary publication devoted to the Great Exhibition. Baccarat and Saint-Louis did not exhibit.

Again in 1853 Baccarat and Saint-Louis did not exhibit at the New York Crystal Palace Exhibition, but Clichy "paperweights of crown glass" were listed in the Official Catalogue. Praising the Clichy exhibit, Horace

Greeley wrote, "The collection of Mr. Maez [Maës] of Clichy is a very extensive and beautiful one . . . not only is the ornamentation and coloring of Mr. Maez's collection of great merit, but in the design and form of the vessels there is great taste . . . . The paperweights, already alluded to, are here in innumerable variety."

There are magnificent performances from all three French factories, and each had its own specialty; but considered as a whole, Clichy paperweights show more imagination in variety of design as, for instance, in the almost endless variety of garland patterns. The patterns and ruffled shapes of the millefiori canes are more interesting and their colors appear richer than those of the other two factories, especially when set into brilliantly colored grounds. The lampworked single flowers are strikingly individual, and the floral bouquets, often tied with glass ribbons, are more naturally disposed within the glass. Even Clichy's leaves show a variety of shapes, colors, and veining that contrasts with the stiff, formally posed, and endlessly repeated leaves from Baccarat and Saint-Louis that are placed in assigned groupings about flowers that look as if they were pressed in a book. Clichy weights, always brilliant, usually superbly executed, epitomize the best in the decorative arts.

In America, as in France, there is ample proof that glass paperweights were made commercially and in quantity, especially by the New England Glass Company and the Boston & Sandwich Glass Company from 1852, when dated examples appear, through the 1870's. In their scholarly books discussing the products of these factories, both Lura Woodside Watkins and Kenneth M. Wilson have contributed solid proof of this production in the form of letters, company invoices, and price lists. American paperweights were frequently made by emigrés from England and the Continent, some of whom had served their apprenticeships at Baccarat, Saint-Louis, and Murano. They copied both strictly and with variations such well-known French paperweight flowers as the Baccarat clematis, wheatflower, and buttercup, and made liberal use of Saint-Louis jasper grounds, and of Saint-Louis and Clichy latticed grounds, often called baskets. A limited number—probably not more than one hundred—of concentric and carpet ground millefiori paperweights were also made at the Gillinder factory in Philadelphia during the decade 1861-1871 and are among the loveliest of all American weights. A small number of large paperweights containing lampworked roses, other flowers and fruits, and butterflies were made at the Mount Washington Glass Company of New Bedford, Massachusetts, during the 1870's. Mount Washington paperweights are mentioned as being included in the factory's exhibit at the Centennial Exposition in Philadelphia in 1876.

Collecting paperweights is nothing new. When paperweights were being produced during the 1840's, they were seen by a widely traveling public at exhibitions in Paris, Vienna, London, Birmingham, and elsewhere, purchased for a pittance from the various factory outlets, and carried home as souvenirs. A rare overlay weight, recently sold at auction, had descended in the family of a London streetsweeper.

It is not known when weights first began to be collected by royalty and the nobility. The Emperor Napoleon III's wife, the Princess Eugénie, the Princess Murat, and the Duke of Cardoza were all collectors, as was the Empress Carlotta, that unfortunate wife of Emperor Maximilian of Mexico—which, incidentally, accounts for the large number of fine paperweights still to be found in Mexican collections. In the famous novel, *Nana* (1880), Emile Zola says of the Count Muffat that he "posted himself in front of a stationer's where with profound attention he contemplated an array of paperweights. . . ." The Royal Collections of England include paperweights which belonged to Queen Mary and may have originally been collected by Queen Victoria, who visited the Crystal Palace Exhibition nearly every day and was given a present on many of her visits. In fact, a paperweight appears on a table in Victoria's sitting room at Old Balmoral in a watercolor done in 1853.

Paperweight collecting spread as the British and French Empires expanded, finding its way to such far-flung places as Spain, Mexico, a palace on a lake in India, and even the remote island of Mauritius in the Indian Ocean, where there are still a few fine collections dating from the period of French rule. In later decades the social and literary notables took a fancy to paperweights—Oscar Wilde and Colette, for example; part of the latter's collection eventually was given to an admiring Truman Capote. During the first half of the twentieth century collecting broadened to include just about anyone with a genuine interest—it might be a socialite, King Farouk, or an American businessman.

It didn't take much money to collect in the early decades of this century. In one of the first Sotheby sales to include paperweights (December 17, 1925), eighty-two weights were offered as a single lot but did not make the reserve and were then sold individually. They sold for a total of $588. By 1929, sale lots were reduced to six, four, or only two weights each, which usually brought less than five pounds per lot. In 1936, dated Baccarat weights were still bringing less than ten pounds at Sotheby's. Olga Drexel Dahlgren's now famous French lily-of-the-valley on translucent cranberry red ground (p. 71, No. 201), which fetched $20,400 in the recession year of 1970, cost Miss Dahlgren less than $100 when she bought the weight about 1930. The real boom in paperweight collecting, and therefore in paperweight prices, did not begin until after the end of World War II. Today, with books, magazine articles, and sales catalogues to guide them, there are hundreds of collectors all over the world, some with substantial collections both in quantity and quality.

Unfortunately for a growing number of serious collectors, not only are prices for the finer weights rising steeply, but the market is shrinking. An old friend of mine, Mrs. Viola Neiman, volunteered recently to record the number of glass paperweights and related millefiori or lamp-worked objects appearing in Sotheby catalogues. Her tally shows that from 1951 through early 1974, a period of nearly a quarter century, and by far the most active period for paperweight sales, the total number of paperweights and related objects offered for sale by Sotheby's was only 3,245. Of these, 1,186 were catalogued as Baccarat, 1,100 as Clichy, and only 959 as coming from the Saint-Louis factory. While this may come as a surprise to those who assume that there are many thousands of antique glass paperweights waiting to be purchased, it should surprise no one that, year by year, fine collections are being donated to museums, thus removing them from the marketplace. As this is being written, a collection of approximately one thousand classic period paperweights is being given to The Art Institute of Chicago.

Time has also taken its toll. A weight subjected to changes in temperature just sitting on a windowsill may yield to an unsuspected and invisible annealing stress, burst with a loud report, and be found in two pieces on the floor. There have been instances at antique shows where the glass shelf of a dealer's display cabinet, loaded with paperweights, has given way, smashing many of the weights. During a paperweight exhibition in a museum some years ago, an improperly installed and overloaded thin glass shelf crashed onto the shelf below it, bringing both shelves down onto a third layer of paperweights, thus obliterating or seriously damaging thirty-five weights. One paperweight collection melted in a house fire. Before their value soared, paperweights were often given to children to play with, or even used to drive picture nails into the wall.

By far the most damage to glass paperweights, however, is caused innocently and in ignorance by collectors and dealers who think their weights can be improved by what they like to refer to as "polishing." Polishing can do no more than brighten the surface of a weight. It cannot remove deep scratches, bruises, chips, or other blemishes which go beneath the skin of weights and which the paperweight owner, prospective purchaser, or dealer who sells the weight, each for his own special reason, considers unsightly; "polishing" is simply a euphemism for grinding. Less than total grinding leaves flat places that distort the design. Proper grinding, however justified and however correctly and tenderly done, necessarily removes a layer of glass from the entire curved surface of the paperweight, not just the damaged area. In so doing it alters the original magnification of the glass dome, changing what was meant to be seen. Grinding often so changes the view from the top down *into* the paperweight that parts of the actual design—the tips of lampworked leaves, for example, or an outer ring of canes—disappear when looked at from above, and the perimeter of the design often becomes blurry. No scrupulous person would think of tampering with ancient glass to *improve* it, but when it comes to antique glass paperweights, few aficionados—and this includes museums—seem aware of the irreversible alterations on paperweights they authorize or tolerate. It is safe to say that only a very small percentage of classic period paperweights look today as they were intended to look when they were produced in the mid-nineteenth century. A paperweight simply cannot be restored by removing part of it, and most old weights are better left with their knocks and abrasions of time.

## IN CONCLUSION

**M**ost of the significant developments and techniques in the history of glassmaking—millefiori and filigree cane making, lampwork, the uses of color and design, lead formulas, blocking and shaping, even blowing (as in the case of crown weights), annealing, cutting, gilding, enameling, incrustation—come together in classic paperweight making. The paperweight form is one of nearly perfect circularity that contains the most complex of designs yet translates the simplest of designs into infinity. Add to this the mystery created by the magnifying convex dome—the tantalizing, intangible mystery of what is really inside the weight—and the equally mysterious reduction of the design produced by concave cutting, and, finally, the kaleidoscopic multiplication and fragmentation of the design achieved through complicated faceting, and one comes to understand why glass paperweights are different from all other glass forms. For these crystal balls contain both the questions and the answers. In their wonderful size relationship to the human hand, their heavy shape and shaped weight, their brilliance yet delicacy, glass paperweights of the classic period are truly the crown jewels of collecting.

Paul Hollister

## CLOSE MILLEFIORI

Industrial technologies of the mid-nineteenth century permitted the imitation of any and all decorative styles of the past and, indeed, encouraged their over-elaboration. In glass, as in everything else, taste was eclectic. With overwhelming success, a number of Venetian, French, German, and Bohemian glassmakers attempted to reproduce the ancient patterns achieved by drawing out hot glass canes incorporating a continuous design that could be sliced into repetitions of itself almost ad infinitum, like slices from a carrot or cucumber. The visual effect of arrangements of cane slices was well described in nineteenth-century coinage of the term *mille fiori*, Italian for *thousand flowers*. Closely packed millefiori designs like those shown on the first two plates are the simplest and perhaps the most effective designs found in glass paperweights of the Classic Period. One can study these close millefiori designs over and over and still find something new.

## VENETIAN BALL

Page 26 shows a Venetian Renaissance millefiori ball with an inclusion in the form of a *lattimo* (opaque-white) glass fragment bearing an enameled portrait of a young man in the style of Carpaccio. The *lattimo* fragment, which must have remained from a broken cup or bowl datable to the decade 1500-1510, was most likely retrieved from the glasshouse floor and picked up in the millefiori gather that formed the ball. The ball itself reminds us of Sabellico's observation made about 1494 (See p. 13).

Weight No. 2 (p. 26) is a nineteenth-century paperweight version of the Venetian ball, signed and dated POB 1845 (for Pietro Bigaglia). Note how close the millefiori canes are to the surface of the weight, as they are in No. 162 (p. 27) from the French Saint-Louis factory, undated, but probably made in 1845. Enameled foil flowers make No. 297 (p. 26) a rare weight, but the cane clusters are unlike those associated with any specific factory.

No. 163 (p. 27) is an unusually large, finely compacted, egg-shaped handcooler with a cane centered in the blunter end. This cane must have been difficult to place, since that end appears to have been where the pontil rod was attached while the handcooler was being made.

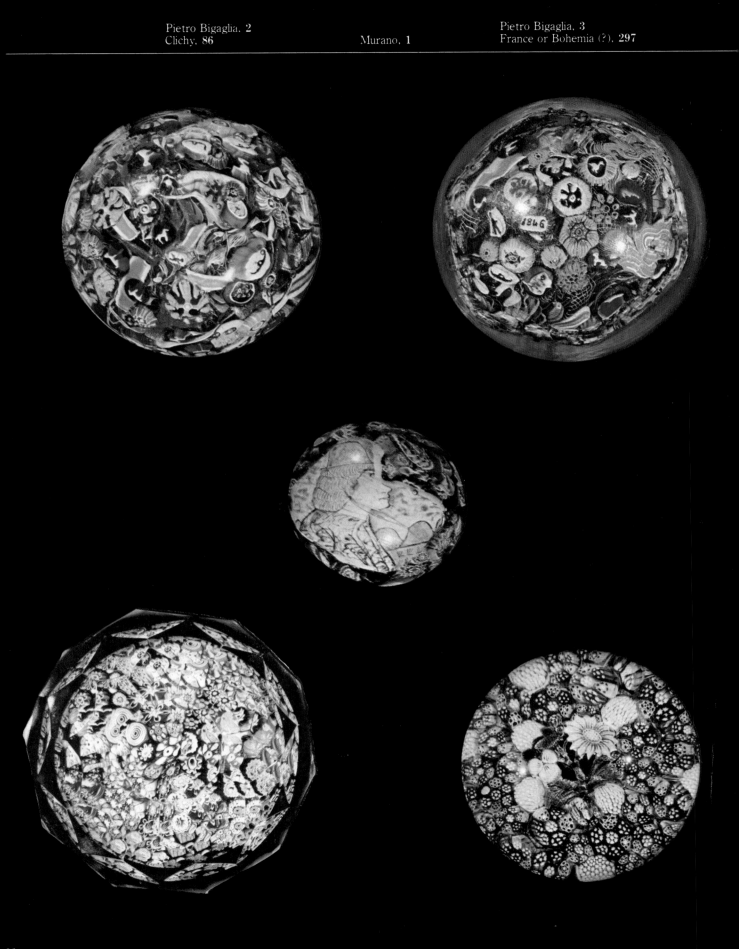

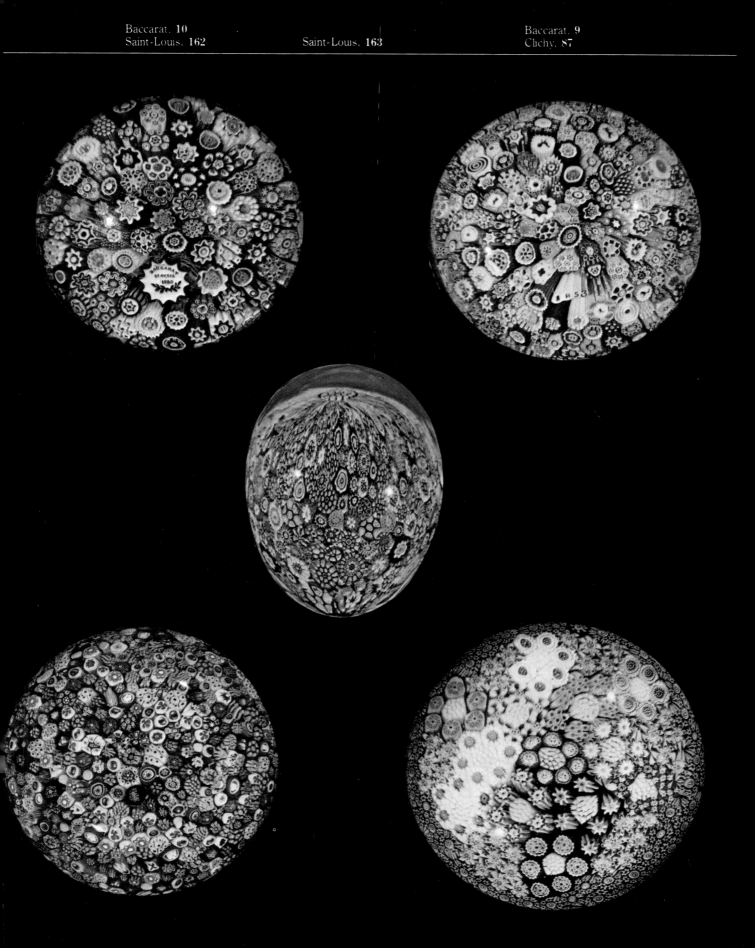

## SPACED CONCENTRICS

Spaced concentric arrangements are placed over many different types of ground. Though No. 89 (p. 29) is the only recorded example from a French factory of a latticed ground with a colored middle layer, several American examples are known, indicating that in this instance the influence may have traveled from West to East. The square canes of No. 90 (p. 29) are seldom seen. Double overlays Nos. 4 and 5 (p. 30) from Bohemia are rare, surprising, especially since overlaying (casing) was a Bohemian specialty. The centered Baccarat rose in Weight No. 12 (p. 30) is also rare, since a differently shaded pink rose, similar in form, is considered the trademark of Clichy paperweights.

## CARPET GROUNDS

Carpet grounds, usually associated with clustered paperweight designs, are among the most appealing foils for colored and silhouette canes. Carpets formed of sparkling white stardust canes make brilliant settings in which the colored canes stand out like gems. Only four stardust carpets are known from Clichy, and of these No. 95 (p. 31) is the subtlest and most delicate of fancies. The moss ground No. 93 (p. 32) is signed CLICHY on the reverse, a rarity added to the rarity of its having a moss ground. Note the subtle tonalities of Baccarat No. 36 (p. 33) with its hundreds of tiny shamrock rods. Note the effective simplicity of No. 172 (p. 33). The few known carpet grounds from Gillinder & Sons, Philadelphia, look soft as feathers, as will be apparent from No. 265 (p. 34). By contrast, No. 247 (p. 34) from the New England Glass Company of East Cambridge, Massachusetts, is peppermint sharp. Saint-Louis produced divided or paneled carpets such as No. 168 (p. 35) with Empress Josephine, another containing a pansy sulphide (167, p. 35), and one of two recorded concentric "tricolore" carpets (169, p. 36), which make an interesting contrast to the Bacchus concentric No. 240. Hexagonal color fields were a Clichy specialty (No. 108, p. 36).

The question, When is a carpet ground not a carpet ground? is posed by concentrics 99 and 176 (p. 37). Even when Saint-Louis concentrics lack the precision of Clichy and Baccarat they are interesting. Bacchus 239 (p. 36) is not a carpet ground: the "sodden snow"-white is really seven glass life-savers inserted to contain the groups of canes.

## CHECKERS

Among the checker patterns, No. 16 (p. 39) with turquoise grid is the rarest, and perhaps also the least subtle. Clichy checkers (92) make attractive newel ornaments.

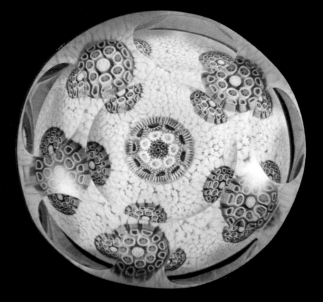

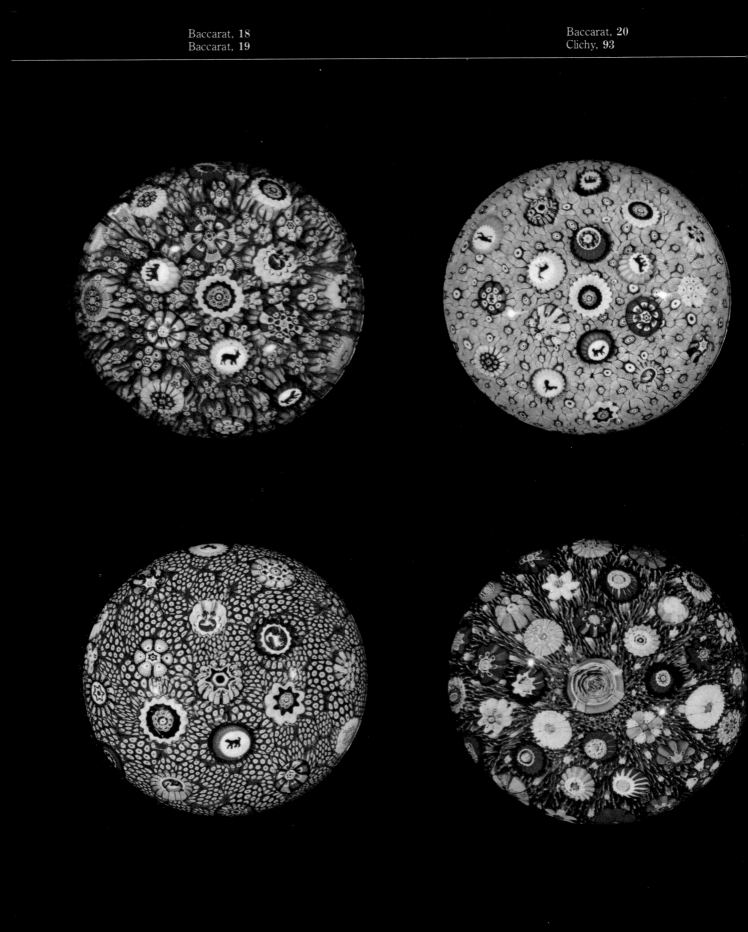

Baccarat, 36
Saint-Louis, 173
Saint-Louis, 174

Baccarat, 35
Saint-Louis, 175
Saint-Louis, 172

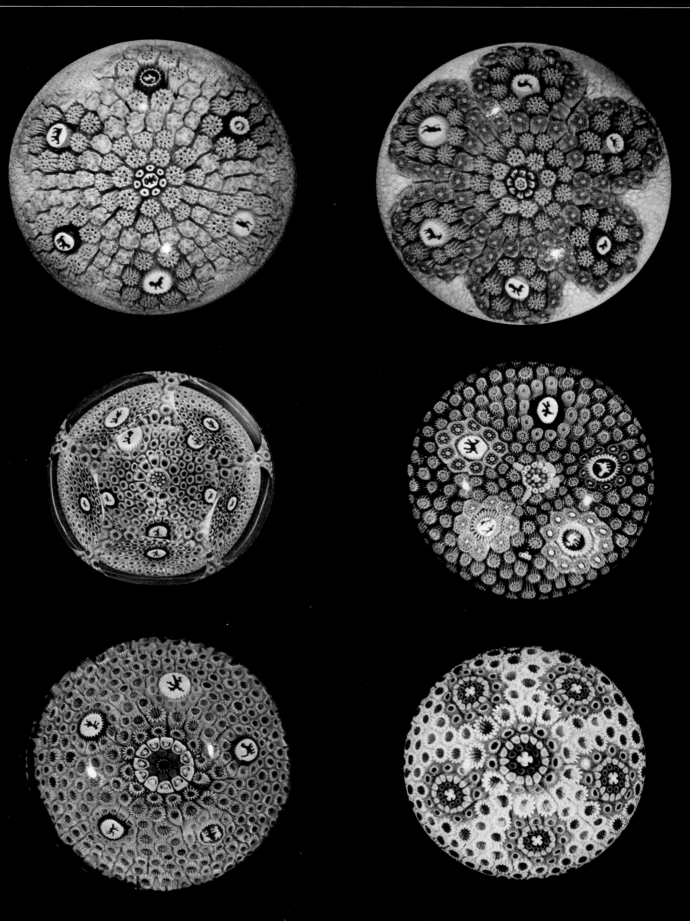

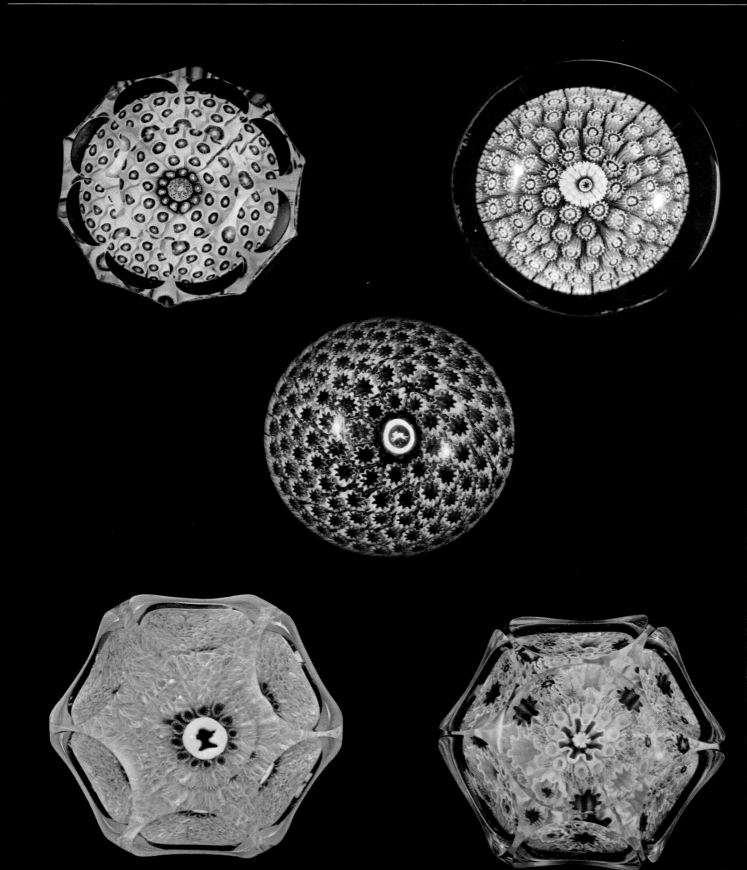

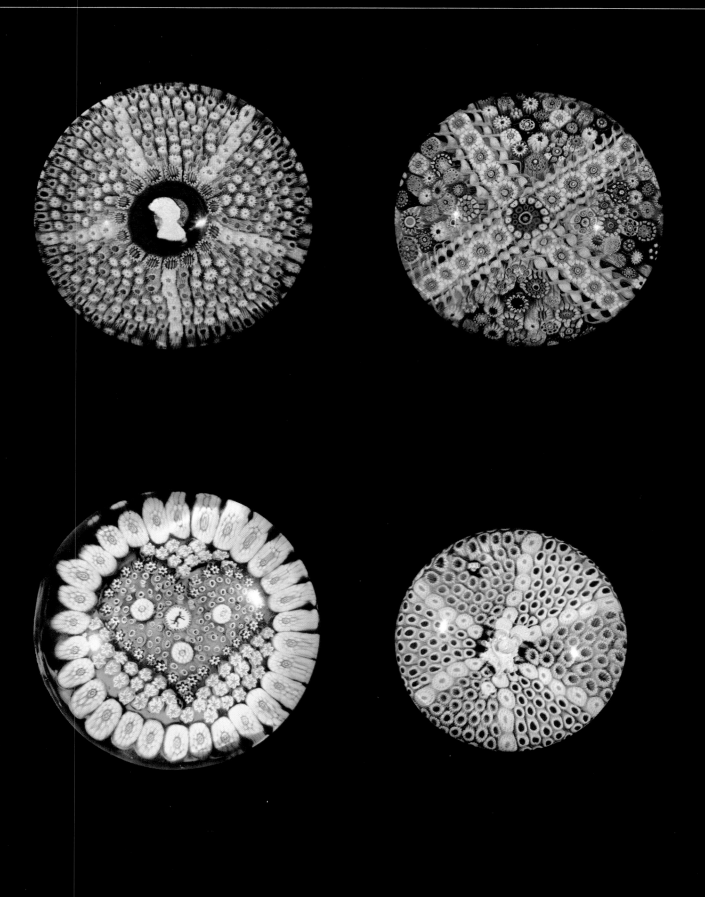

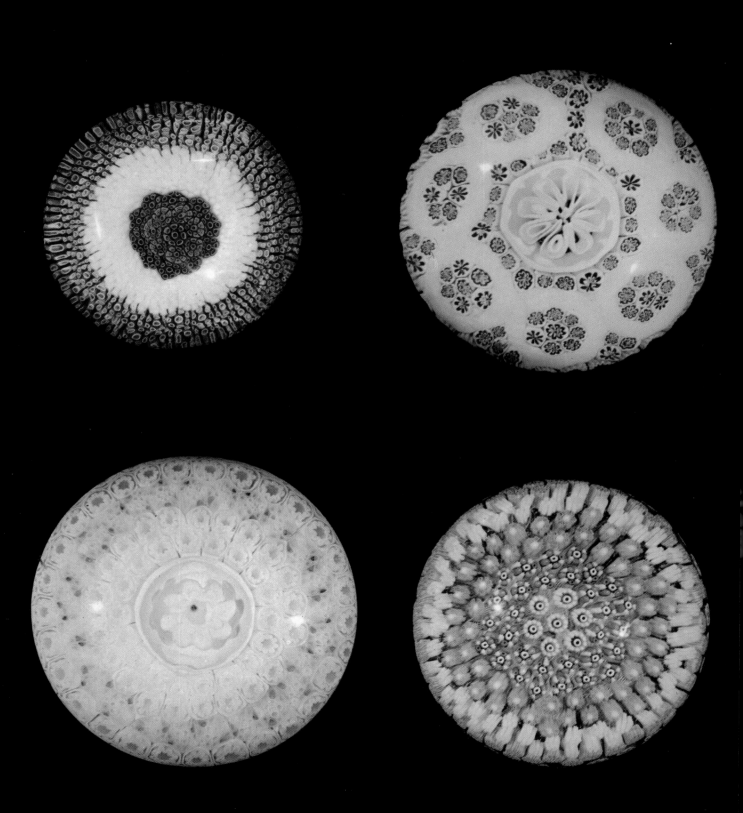

## BASKETS

Though it once had a free-standing filigree handle, No. 120 (p. 41) is still one of the most adventurous and marvelous weights ever made. Possibly it is unique. The Clichy gaffer who made it may have tried to go the Saint-Louis enclosed basket one better. Enclosed stave baskets with handles were obviously a technical challenge. The staves used for the basket sides were a device to mask čanes that were cut of irregularly on the bottom instead of being drawn to the base of the weight. Nos. 6 and 7 (p. 42) are rare Bohemian baskets, while p. 43 shows pedestal examples from the three French factories. The gilded metal base of No. 100 furnishes the earliest date (1845) associated with Clichy.

## MUSHROOMS

One of the most popular paperweight forms, that of the nosegay or bridal bouquet (See the virgin, No. 22, p. 46), has been given the pedestrian name of mushroom. Mushrooms were produced by the three big French factories, in Bohemia, and by Bacchus in England; they came with and without *torsades*. The base might be amber-flashed, cross-hatched, star- or petal-cut, according to factory styles. Circles composed of roses, favored by Clichy, enhanced the sense of bouquet, and even Baccarat (23, p. 46) sometimes included them. Weight No. 241 (p. 45) from Bacchus is exceptionally well done, including the *torsade*, which was achieved without the circular bubble that often plagued Baccarat and Saint-   s *torsades*. Perhaps that is why Clichy left out the *torsade*. But many overlaid Clichy mushrooms show an unwanted bubble just above the base. Such Clichy overlay colors as the soft eggshell (105) and the forest green (106, p. 47) are exceptional.

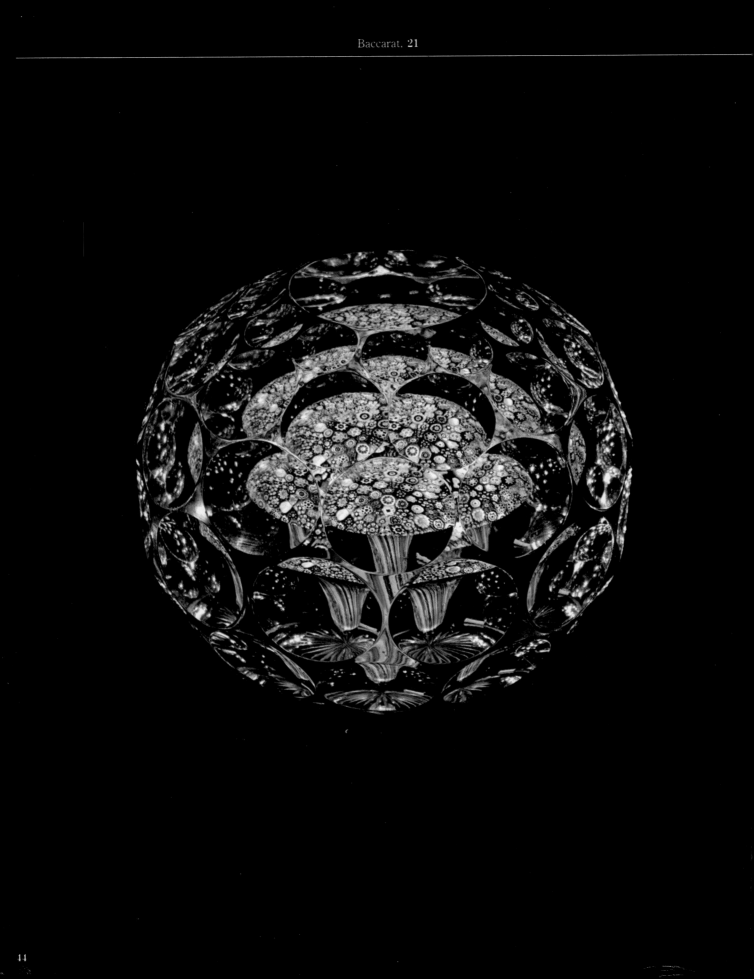

Baccarat, **22**
Baccarat, **23**
Baccarat, **24**

Saint-Louis, **180**
Saint-Louis, **179**
Saint-Louis, **181**

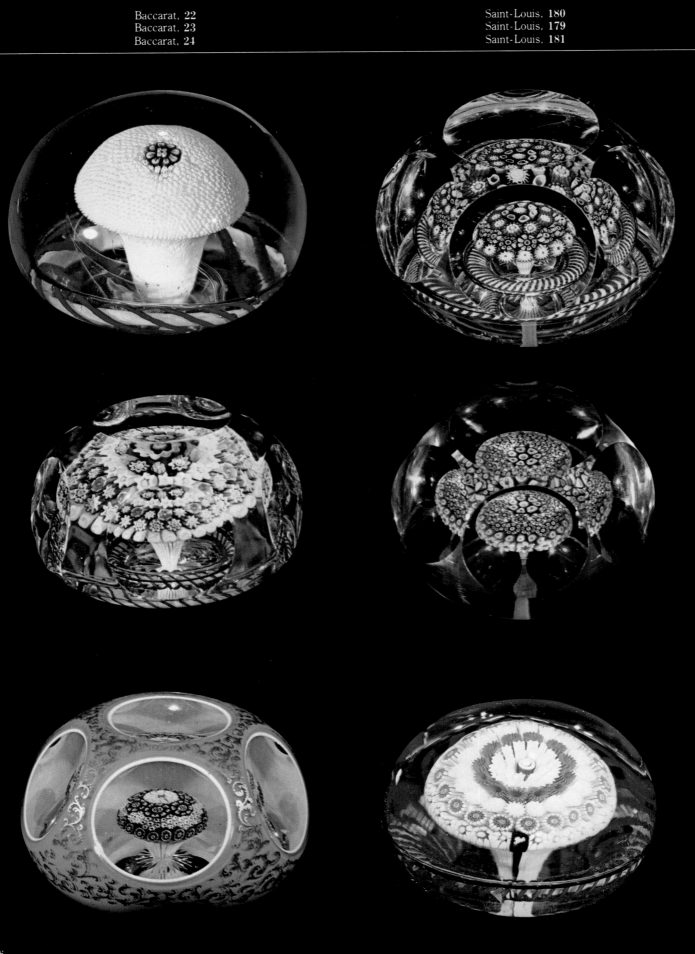

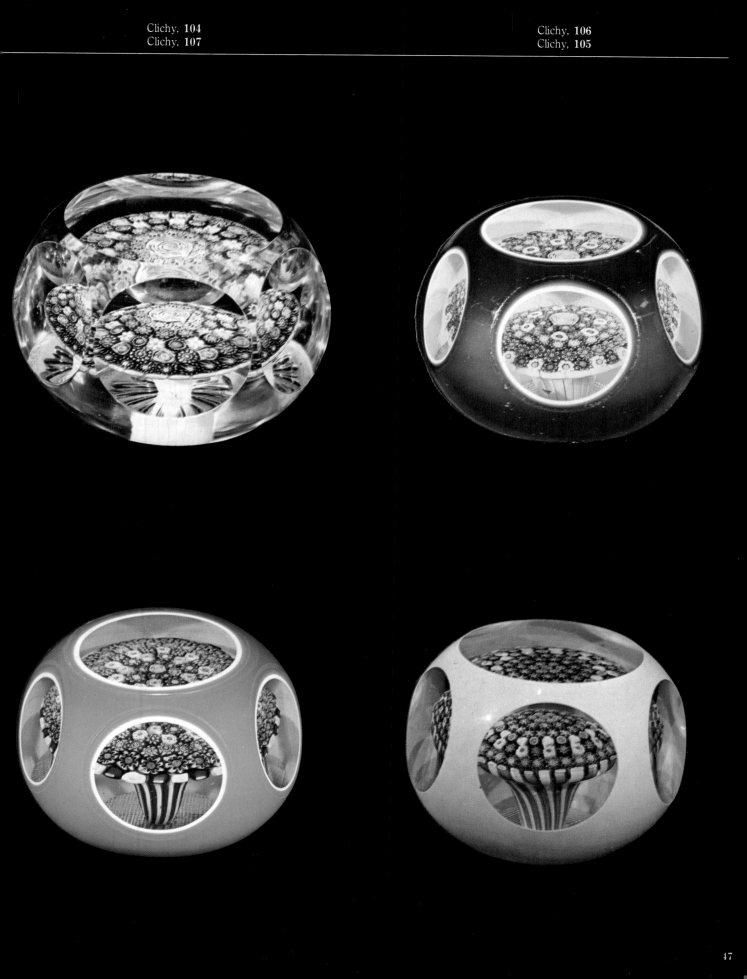

Perhaps the most varied and exacting millefiori designs were the garlands. Apart from the outstanding Baccarat examples shown here, Nos. 27, 28, 29 and 33 (pp. 49, 50), for example, imitating the Clichy star, Baccarat and also Saint-Louis garlands seem to have been generally perfunctory exercises, as if their makers were content to let Clichy walk away with vibrant interwoven strands, multiple loops, and C-scroll designs on fluffy lace and brilliant color grounds. The double overlay of Baccarat 32 (p. 50), though done to perfection, nevertheless obscures the interior design because that design was not set in a color ground, whereas in No. 31 (p. 50) similar interlocked trefoils stand out against the coral texture of the stardust ground. The sulphide and enameled motifs in Nos. 116 and 161 (p. 51) make these weights excessively rare. All in all, Clichy paperweights represent the best in classic paperweight making.

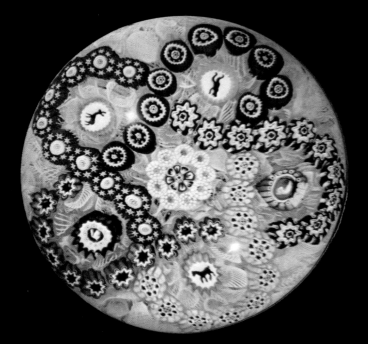

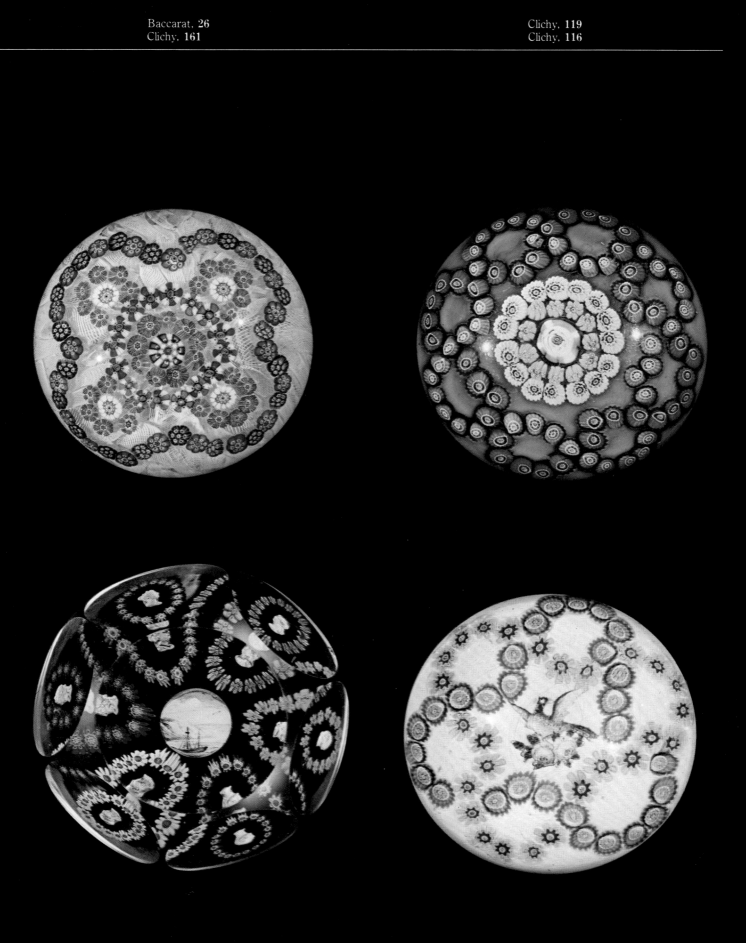

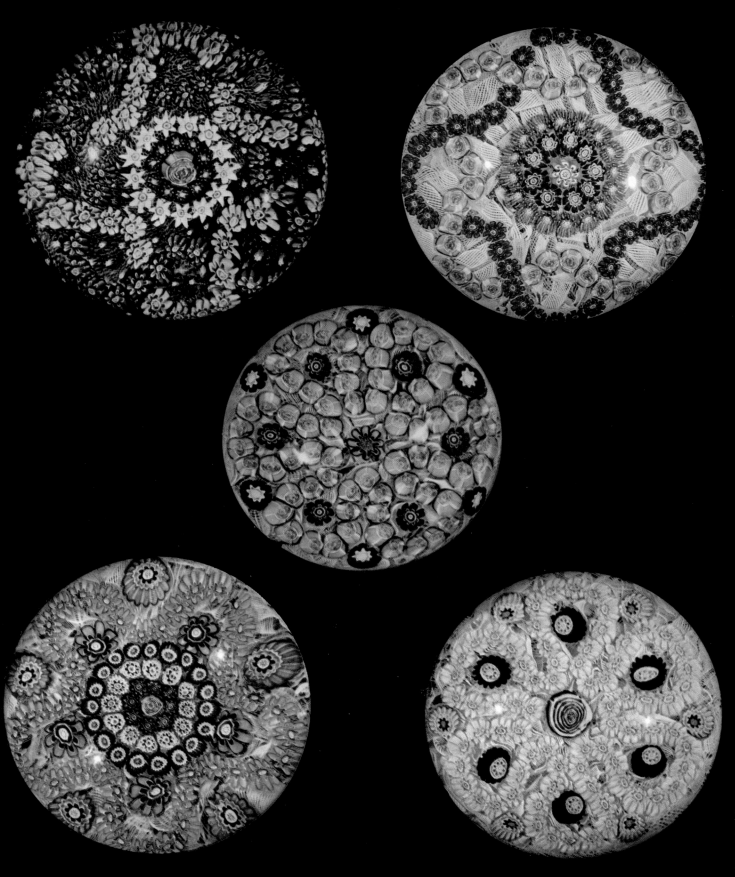

Swirls were another Clichy specialty, just the hollow blown marbrie was for Saint-Louis. Tightly spiraled swirls such as Nos. 121 or 122 (p. 55) especially when centered by a Clichy rose, are much sought after. Often the spiraled strands are spread too far apart, revealing bubbles that disturb the eye. The patriotic red, white, and blue of No. 123 (p. 55), and especially the starred center, suggest that the weight was perhaps intended as a subtle reminder of American liberty during the French Revolution of 1848. Marbries like No. 189 (p. 55) look as if they were difficult to make. Another Saint-Louis marbrie appears beneath a molded lizard (233, p.106).

## CROWNS

Notwithstanding a few Bohemian examples (8, p. 56), hollow blown crowns were a Saint-Louis trademark, copied with variations by the Boston & Sandwich and the New England Glass companies in America. Yellow aventurine ribbons make No.186 rare, but not as rare as the paired and neatly twisted red and blue ribbons of No.184 (p. 56), which would seem to have been a happy variation on the crown theme, perhaps made up as a special order. Festive No. 188 (p. 57), complete with its own pedestal, may have been inspired by one of the Montgolfier balloons with gondola.

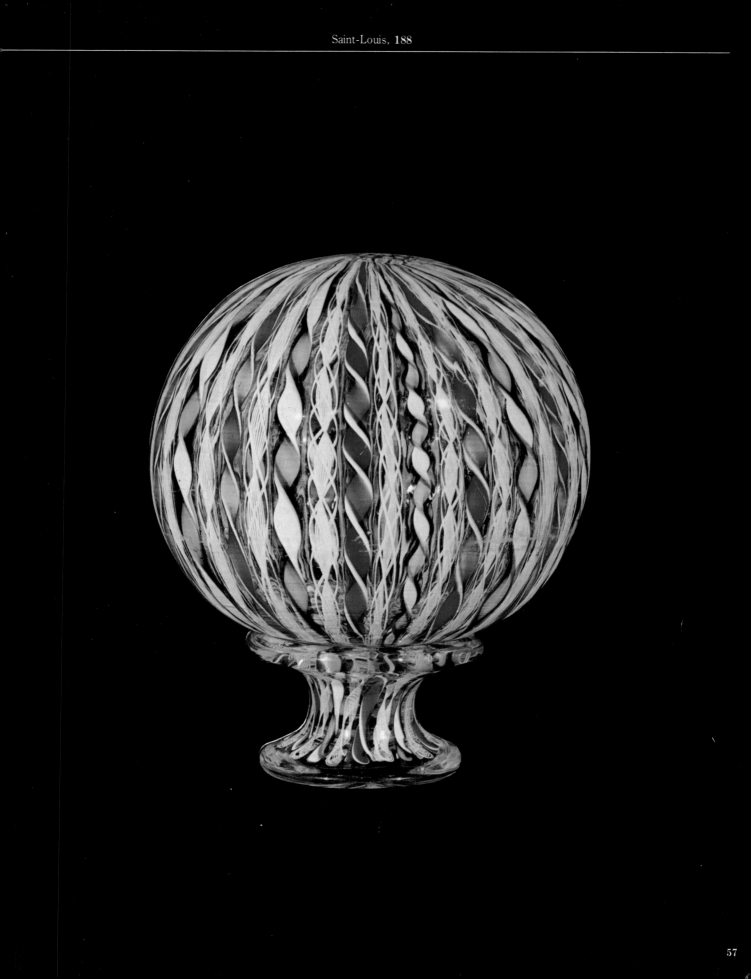

## FLAT POSIES

In all paperweight floral arrangements the adjective "flat" is used to denote designs in which the flower or flowers, or the canes representing blossoms are placed flat or on a slightly curved bed of glass. Flat posies combine millefiori canes with lampworked leaves. French examples from Saint-Louis are more relaxed in execution than their stiff, antler-like American counterparts. Weight No. 192 (p. 61) is an early Saint-Louis arrangement on snow ground that was soon to be abandoned for a set design of four canes, four leaves, and curved stem centered in a variety of cut and amber-flashed settings. This simple formula is dramatically reduced in size by concave faceting in No. 251 (p. 60), in which the brilliantly cut, almost bizarre black (actually deep purple-blue) over opaque white double overlay frames the posy as if it were an aria sung on the stage of a great opera house. Few flat flowers appeal to the collector more than the Clichy rose, shown to best advantage in the miniature No. 124 and with other blossoms in the rare No. 145 (p. 61).

## SINGLE FLAT FLOWERS

Flat single flowers from Clichy are rare, while Baccarat and Saint-Louis apparently thrived on unlimited editions of the pansy, clematis, primrose, pompon, and others. However, all the paperweight flowers in this exhibition are unusual or rare in coloring or some other aspect, and most are beautiful as works in glass. Compare the neatly executed Baccarat wheatflower No. 51 (p. 65) with its less neat Sandwich version 260, or the laminated petals of Baccarat 49 (p. 63) with its even more intricate Val Saint-Lambert counterpart, No. 277.

Many, perhaps most, paperweight flowers are only loosely derived from botanical varieties. Whatever they represent, such flowers as Nos. 48, 50, and 53 (pp. 63, 65) with its budding blossom, the viola (131, p. 70) within its ring of roses and canes, the tiny fuchsia (205, p. 71), the juicy dahlia (132, p. 68), not to mention the peppermint-striped (196, p. 67), or the twin-bloom (206, p. 71) flowers, the pompon (200, p. 69) on ruby ground, and the cupped, red-petaled No. 42 (p. 64) would be hard to beat, unless it were by the other flowers illustrated. The New England buttercup (253, p. 69) was undoubtedly made by someone who had seen the Baccarat version. The remarkable inventiveness of Clichy flowers is well shown in 129 (p . 62). In 139 and 140 (p. 72) the ruffled petals are actually achieved by canes sliced lengthwise like exposed petticoats.

Paperweight flowers are usually composed of preformed, interchangeable parts. Saint-Louis leaves, for example, are nearly always the same bright green with the same toothed edges and ridged veining (produced by a clamp) regardless of flower. The same is true for Sandwich leaves which, though deeper green, resemble their prototypes. Baccarat uses only two kinds of leaves: pinnately compound and linear. One interesting flower, No. 266 (p. 66), doubtless meant to represent a poinsettia, appropriately shows the Mount Washington veining, produced by the same clamp, on both leaves and petals.

Saint-Louis and Clichy dahlias, Saint-Louis and Baccarat pompons, Baccarat and New England buttercups, and some imaginative Clichy flowers also show a degree of three-dimensional relief.

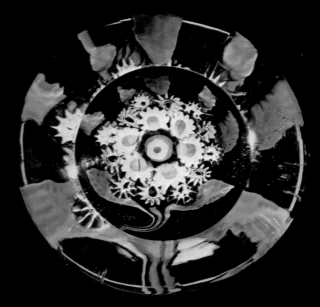

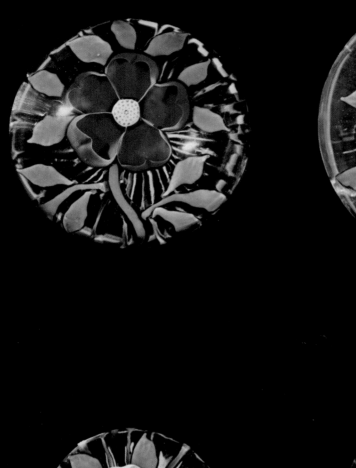

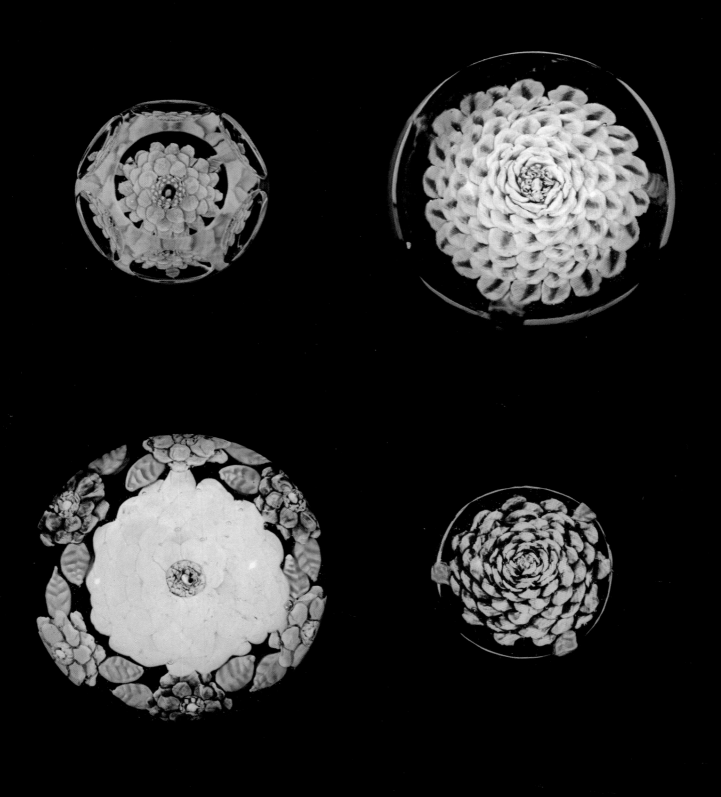

Saint-Louis, 200
Saint-Louis, 199
Saint-Louis, 198

Baccarat, 56
New England Glass Company, 253
Baccarat, 57

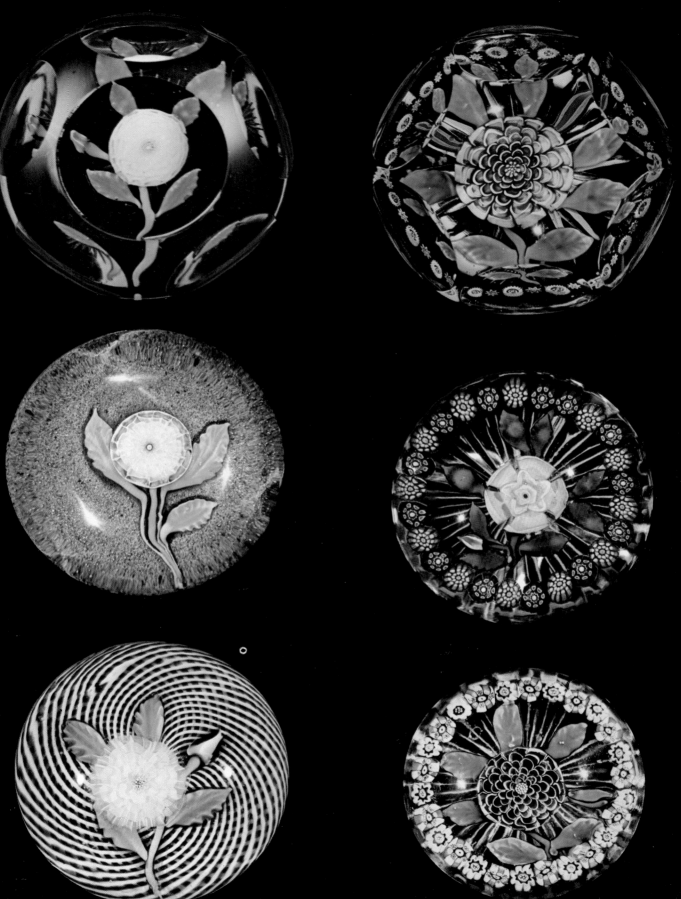

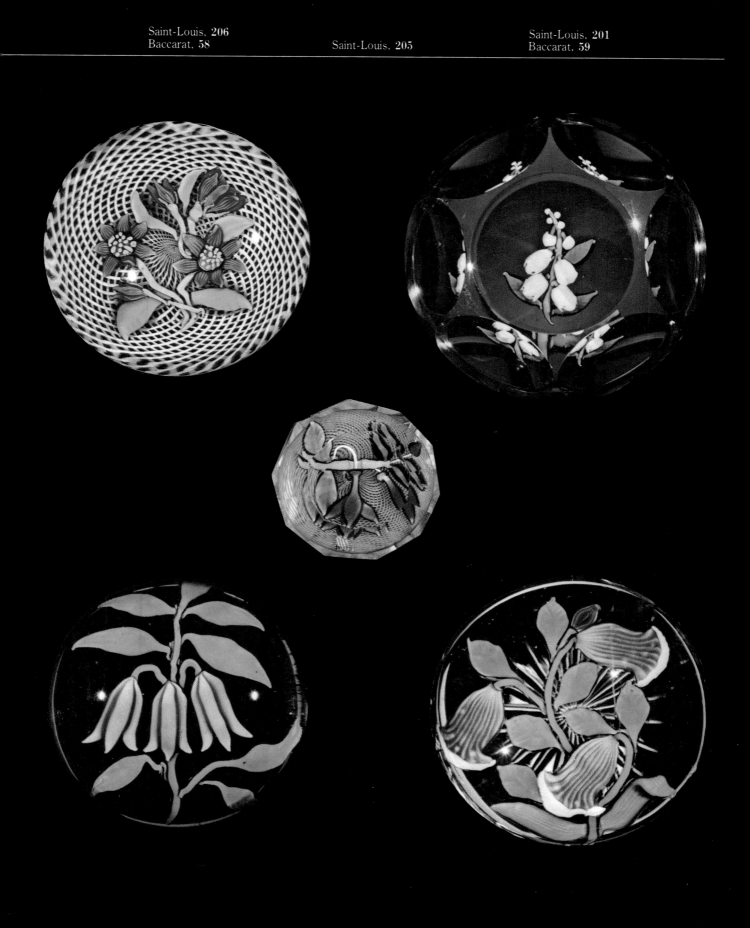

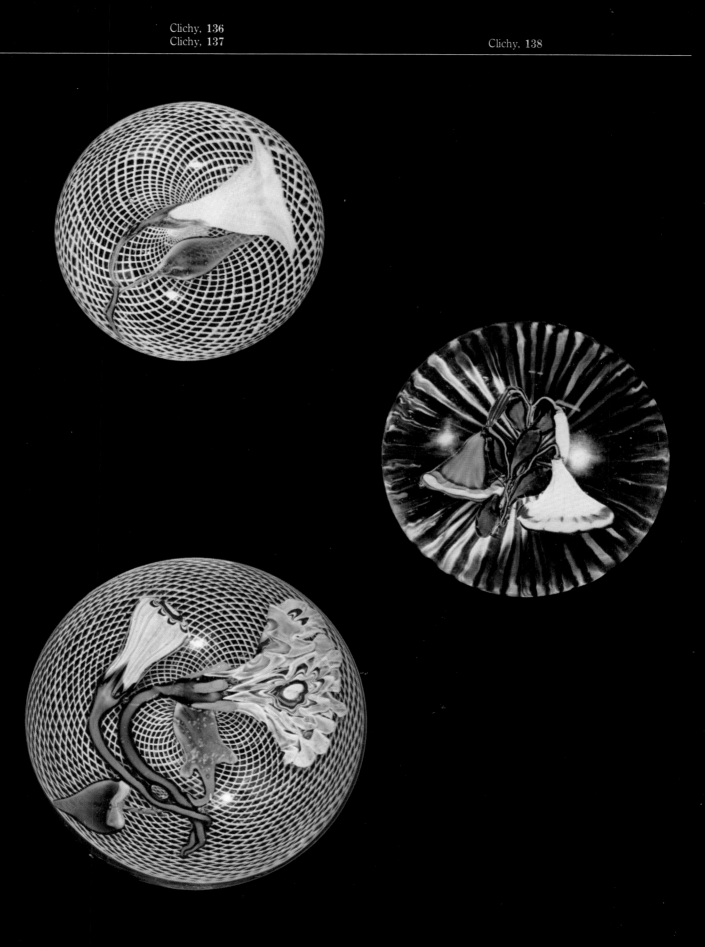

Like single flowers, flat floral bouquets include those arrangements where three or more flowers are laid flat on a clear gather, or on-or-slightly above a colored or latticed ground. As will be evident in comparing Baccarats 60 and 61 (p. 75) with Clichy 148, 150 (p. 77), Baccarat floral arrangements are formal, where Clichy appear casual, improvisational, like flowers just picked and held loosely together with ribbon. The formal positioning of the four flowers in No. 60 (p. 75) is repeated with different flowers in No. 64, both groups showing crossed stems, as does No. 66 (p. 75). Even the uncentered but balanced composition (62, p. 75) has the same crossed stems. Saint-Louis 207 (p. 76) represents an arrangement that remains nearly constant, as flowers are substituted. Not content with the usual paperweight form, Clichy also fused single flowers and bouquets to opaline plaques, as in the exquisite bouquet of No. 147 (p. 76). Notice how different in size and texture the flowers look without the magnifying dome.

Nearly all examples of flat floral bouquets show paperweight making at its gayest and most exuberant, belying the Victorian reputation for the lugubrious. Yet even in such company the Clichy bouquets stand out as imaginative masterpieces.

Clichy, 149
Clichy, 150
Clichy, 148

Baccarat, 65
Clichy, 141
Clichy, 144

## THREE-DIMENSIONAL SINGLE FLOWERS

Three-dimensional lampworked flowers represent an illusionary advance, if not a naturalistic one over the flat variety. Petals, stamens, even leaves, no matter how botanically hybrid, suggest real counterparts somewhere in nature and demonstrate the lampworker's imagination and skill. Particular success was achieved in the elimination of unwanted air bubbles, probably without benefit of today's vacuum cups which suck out the air. One marvels at the absence of bubbles, striae, and other interferences in Nos. 288 and 294 (p. 79), whose petals are bowed, whose yellow disks or stamens stand up to support the honeybee.

A rare and convincing upright form made with a metal crimp is the Millville waterlily 274 (p. 79) on footed base, of which fewer than half a dozen are recorded.

## ROSES

Among single flowers from whatever source roses are special in their high relief, whether set under a hollow dome as are 202, 203, 204 from Saint-Louis, or covered with glass like 289 (p. 80). Numbers 291, 292, 293 (p. 81), often attributed to the Pantin factory, are here left unattributed for the reason that no documented Pantin paperweight has turned up for examination. The glass of these paperweights is light in weight, their profiles are high, their basal concavities deep inside rims that show little wear. This excepts them from weights of any known factory of the Classic Period, while the naturalism of the rose suggests a later date.

Among the most spectacular roses immersed in the largest gathers of glass are those made in New Bedford, Massachusetts, after 1869 when the Mount Washington Glass Company was founded. No. 267 (p. 82) is the largest lampworked rose known, while 268 (p. 83) is certainly a candidate for the most beautiful in coloring, reminiscent of the famous Mount Washington Burmese glass and in naturalistic form. Three butterflies hover about the rose in weight 269 (p. 83), its long stem held firmly by a hand wearing a gold wedding band.

Roses from Whitall Tatum Company of Millville, New Jersey, were made not by lampwork but with a metal tool called a crimp. It was shaped like an upright rose and used to force a gather of colored glass up and into the ball of the weight, imparting to the gather in this single action the roselike form of the crimp. No. 275 (p. 82), probably made at Millville by Ralph Barber sometime during the years 1905-1912, is a rose inventively tilted toward the viewer in a large ball of limpid glass above a baluster stem and solid foot, an assembly that must have required at least two persons and a change of pontil rods. Though made long after the close of the Classic Period, it retains a classic elegance.

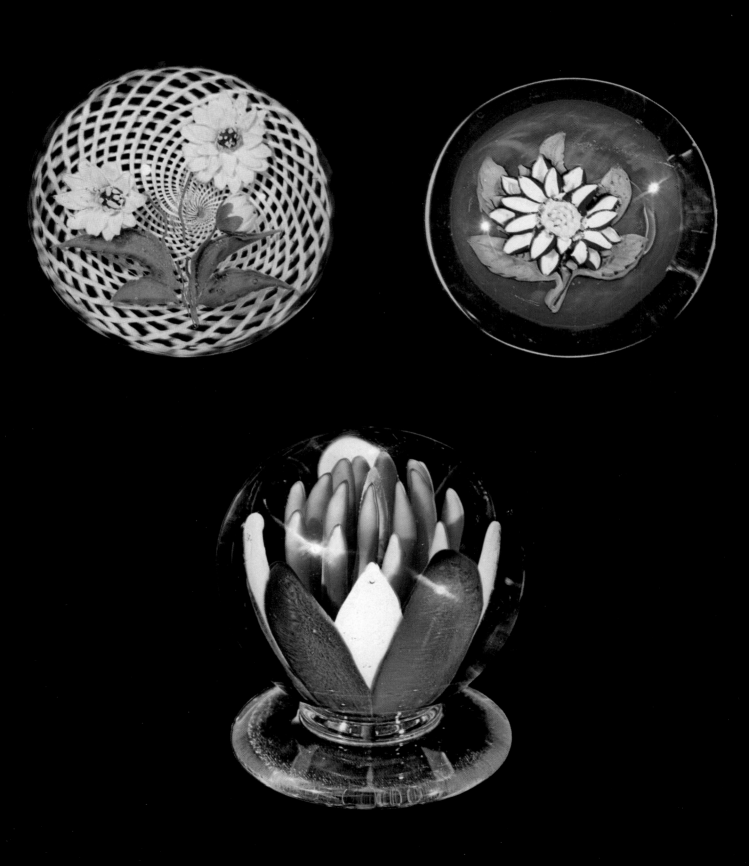

Very few bouquets in relief are known. No. 298 (p. 85) is one in which blue and mauve blossoms, though not markedly sculpted, rest loosely, airily in a yellow basket as if tossed there. A jumble of very three-dimensional wildflowers with gossamer, plumed centers (276) rises, as if from a field, into the high dome of one of the most remarkable and convincing floral paperweights ever made, though its source is unknown. One could almost reach in to pluck a blossom.

Four recorded American examples are the large, massive plaque weights thought to come from Mount Washington. In Weight No. 270 (p. 85) the petals are naturalistically curled and overlapping, the blossoms, leaves, and stems apparently assembled by lampwork in much the same way as a florist's wreath, with threads of glass instead of florist's wire used to join the ensemble. The convincing stems are tied with pleated ribbon, possibly a disguise for a weld to hold the arrangement together during assembly or when it was being covered with hot glass. These spectacular weights probably include more blooms than any other kind.

The upright bouquet, in which flowers and leaves are lampworked into a tall concave funnel or a convex nosegay was a specialty of Saint-Louis, who put them in handcoolers and in weights that were elaborately faceted, overlaid, and encased-overlaid. Some of the more attractive are those in which the bouquet is surrounded by a *torsade* or twisted ribbon beneath multiple facets that break up the design, creating a shifting kaleidoscope as one turns the weight. The problem with a floral relief an inch or two high was to eliminate the air bubbles that could become trapped between leaves and petals, or obscure the colored centers of blossoms. Often Saint-Louis was unsuccessful, particularly in the encased overlays where the visual nuisance that bubbles create is only partly hidden by the overlay.

Encased double overlays, however, are remarkable achievements on any terms. The inner overlaid paperweight had to be annealed and, when cool, faceted like any other overlay weight, often more elaborately. Then the overlaid weight had to be reheated so that an outer covering of clear glass would adhere without cracking the original weight. Care had to be taken not to overheat the weight, or the double overlay might slip under the hot glass covering and lose its painstakingly faceted shape. When one considers the overlay design requirements of weights 211, 216, 217, 221 (pp. 89, 90), or the tricky problem of coating the overlay of 220 with aventurine, or that 215 (p. 89) is a triple overlay—there being a third color inside the white inner overlay—it is no wonder these intricate weights with their illusion of underwater designs are much sought after and very expensive to acquire. The effect of the regular but rare Saint-Louis double overlay 210 (p. 88), not encased, may be contrasted with the many encased examples on exhibit.

Saint-Louis also placed upright bouquets in beautifully fashioned latticed baskets with filigree twist handles (222, 223, p. 91). One of the most remarkable basket weights is No. 224. At some point this weight must have broken, for it has been sliced in half and the rear surface strawberry diamond-cut, a treatment that sets off the basket to perfection.

As rare or rarer than Saint-Louis baskets are the upright bouquets with *torsade* from Baccarat, of which No. 70 (p. 88), with its nicely balanced bouquet and coral *torsade*, is a superb example. Other Baccarat examples manifest the same floral symmetry, a feature noted in the Baccarat flat floral bouquets.

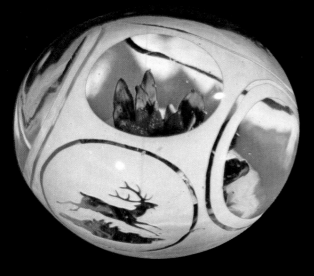

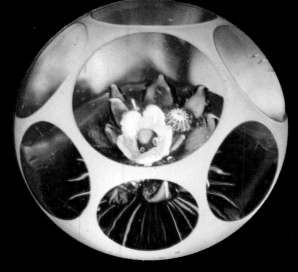

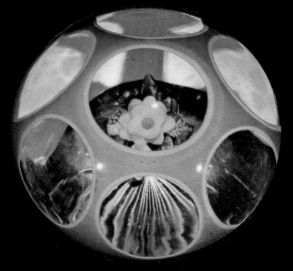

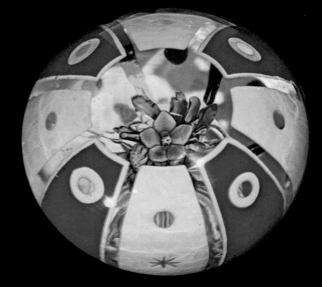

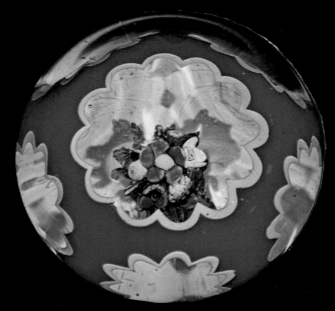

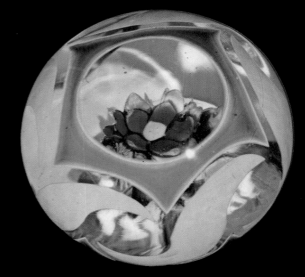

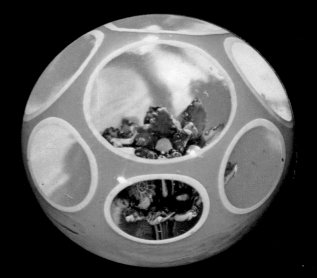

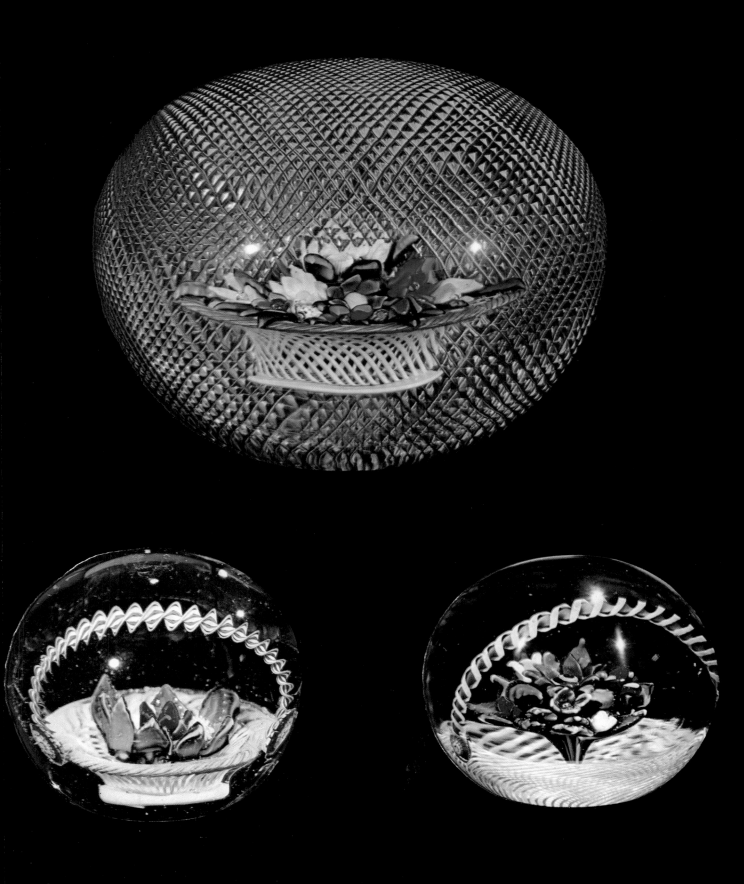

The New England Glass Company also produced upright bouquets on latticed grounds and a variation, the high relief floral sheaf. These usually flawless creations place the bouquet over a latticed, sometimes funnel-shaped ground, often confusingly referred to as a basket, which it is not (255, p. 93). When cutting is applied as surface embellishment the result can be overwhelming as in 256, possibly decorated in a cutting shop outside the factory. The cutter attempted, rather successfully it seems, to compete with the floral interior by placing over the rather formal bouquet a flamboyant mask of leaves. Less in relief but still suspended over the lattice ground is the cross of leaves (254, p. 93) with centered white flower that floats beneath the subtly faceted surface like a floral cross cast into a mountain stream.

Fruits in paperweights, whether composed of solid bundles of hexagonal rods—as are the Baccarat strawberries—or blown like the New England apples and pears, are by process three-dimensional, which may account for the appeal they have for some over flat flower weights.

It is interesting to compare the *fraise du bois* seal No. 272 (p. 96) with strawberry weights 271, 273, all three possibly from Mount Washington, and these in turn with the French 299 (p. 95). The cloudy white hairs like sugar grains on the berries (271) are unlike the opaque yellow grains on the other three examples, and the leaves are differently shaped and pale green. Also, the blossoms are unlike the blossoms in the other weights. No. 271 may well be from another factory, perhaps from Somerville. The single strawberry weight, 305 (p. 95), doubtless has yet another origin.

The truth is many fruit weights have not been sorted out as to origin because there is usually so little visual evidence on which to judge. The leaves, stem, and berries (currants?) of 304 (p. 97) are seen in Saint-Louis flower weights—the berries appear at the top of the stem in fuchsia weights. A Saint-Louis attribution is almost certain. But what about the purple plums or berries in 295 (p. 97), whose high profile and opaque white ground recall some of the unattributed rose weights? And where were the luscious, naturalistic cherries in No. 300 (p. 97) made? Or the wonderful single pear on turkey red ground (296, p. 98) with its unusually convincing leaves—perhaps the most exciting of all fruit weights? We simply do not yet know, and, for exhibition purposes, it does not matter; savoring them is enough. What feats some of them are: the bunch of grapes (225, p. 97) on its diamond-cut ground, the perfect apricots in 71 (p. 95), the primitive painting quality of the wild American fruits (263, p. 97), the delicately shaded New England pears about a flat posy (257, p. 98). An illusion of multiplicity is achieved with just two cherries through thousand-eye faceting in the large and superb No. 226 (p. 97). Illusion is the secret of great paperweight making.

The convincing, life-sized blown fruits from the New England Glass Company were achieved by casings of two or three colors. The large blown and shaped bubble that is weight No. 258 (p.99) was probably rolled on a bed of powdered glass of another color and reblown to produce the apple flecks. That these American fruits derived from earlier French models will be evident from a glance at 232 and at 187 (p. 99) atop a Saint-Louis crown paperweight that was also hollow-blown. The blossom or pontil end of American fruits shows a wad or button of dark green glass, while Saint-Louis examples show an opalescent filigree where the pontil rod was cracked off.

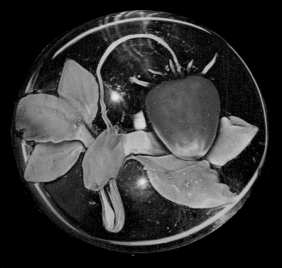

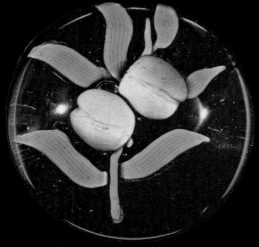

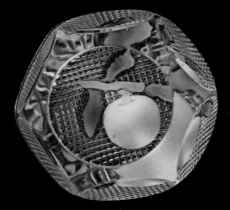

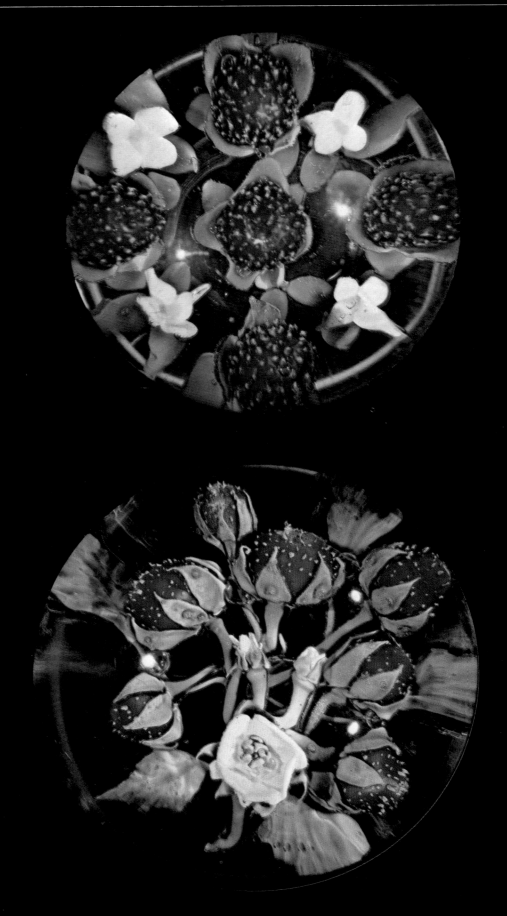

France, unknown, 300
France, unknown, 304

Saint-Louis, 226
Saint-Louis, 225

France, unknown, 295
Boston & Sandwich Glass Company, 263

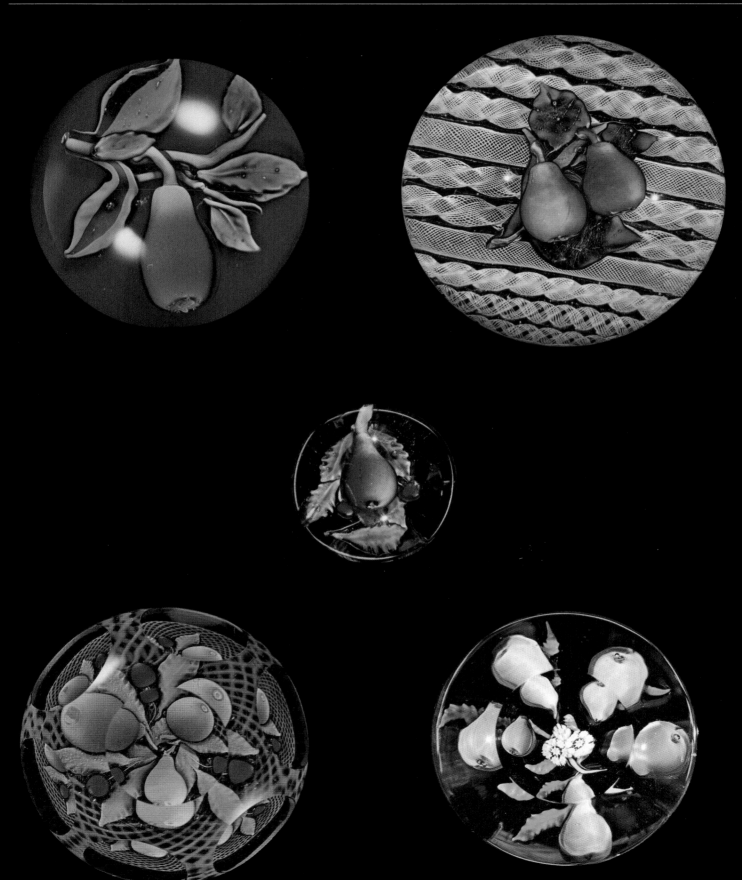

Butterflies placed above flat flowers in a three-dimensional layering process were a Baccarat specialty. Saint-Louis and Clichy produced only a few solo butterflies such as the extremely rare Clichy 153 (p. 101), as interesting on the underside as it is on top. Baccarat 75 (p. 101) shows us a butterfly seen in profile on a flowering stem, thought to be the only such example, though an enameled butterfly in profile is known. No.73 (p. 101) is the only recorded appearance of a butterfly over a color ground set with canes. In No. 231 (p. 102) we have the only known example of a butterfly seen together with a frog.

Other excessively rare fantasies are the swan on a lampworked pond with grassy bank (229, p. 102), the extraordinary flat parrot on a branch of leaves with berries (230, p. 102), and the convincingly sculptural bird on the rim of a nest of blue eggs (290, p. 103). Beside these wonderful paperweights the small blown ducks and swans enclosed in hollow, faceted domes look uninteresting, almost like giftshop novelties, which indeed they were (p. 103).

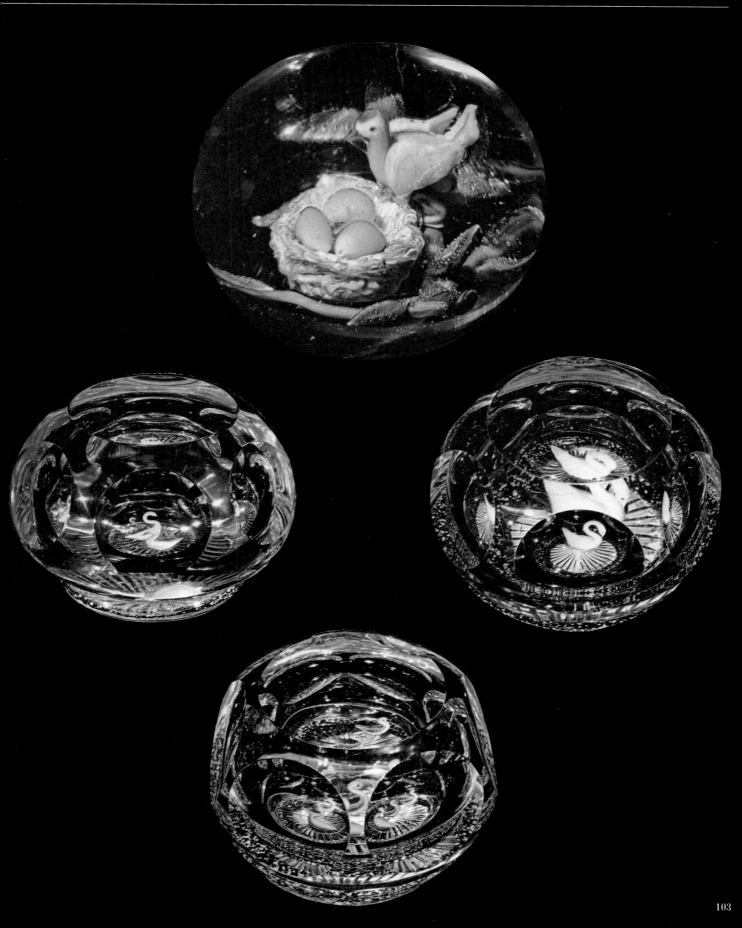

## SNAKES

Snakes from Baccarat and Saint-Louis are always coiled in the same way, their heads with the same harmless smirk. Unlike 76, 77 (p. 105), however, most examples suffer from the same long, trapped air bubbles that afflict the mushroom *torsades* from those factories. The realistic silkworms (weight 287, p. 105) on a leaf above a radiating filigree over blue ground is a triumph of glassmaking that recalls the importance of silk to the nineteenth-century French economy.

## LIZARDS

The molded lizards, 233, 234, 235 (p. 106), coiled atop blown weights were a happy Saint-Louis inspiration. A variety of blown treatments including opaline, cut overlays, marbrie, and jasper, as well as unadorned colored glass adds artistic interest to the zoological accuracy of these specimens, which were formed in the same mold and usually gilded. The lizard in 233 has unfortunately been repainted gold, doubtless because the gilding wore off.

For many the *pièces de résistance* of paperweight collecting are the great lizard *(lézard)* weights in which these saurian reptiles inhabit a convincing environment of sand, moss, and vegetation, including what appear to be aloes flowers. The sand may actually be unfused quartz sand or detritus from the inside of an old glass pot; in 279 and 281 (pp. 108, 109) the sand rests on a ground of opaque white glass the consistency of a cold cream jar. Down among the aloes the lizards—some call them salamanders—present an alert, adventurous posture and a variety of textural detail and markings that may well have been based on particular zoological specimens so popular in the late nineteenth century when the Jardin d'Acclimitation in Paris and other big zoos were a popular attraction. It may be said in passing that a listing of Baccarat paperweights exhibited in 1849 includes the term *zooglyphite* which, according to the *Petit Larousse,* means the fossil imprint of an animal. Lizard weights also appeared in the 1907 price list from Baccarat, and the Colné report of the Paris Exposition of 1878 enumerated "lizards" in the Pantin display of paperweights, including "A paperweight, containing a lizard of colored glass, which had been cut in several parts before being inclosed [sic] in the glass." That factory also gave a "Presse-papier, fleurs et salamandre" (paperweight, flowers and salamander)-an accurate description of precisely these weights-to the Conservatoire des Arts et Métiers in 1880

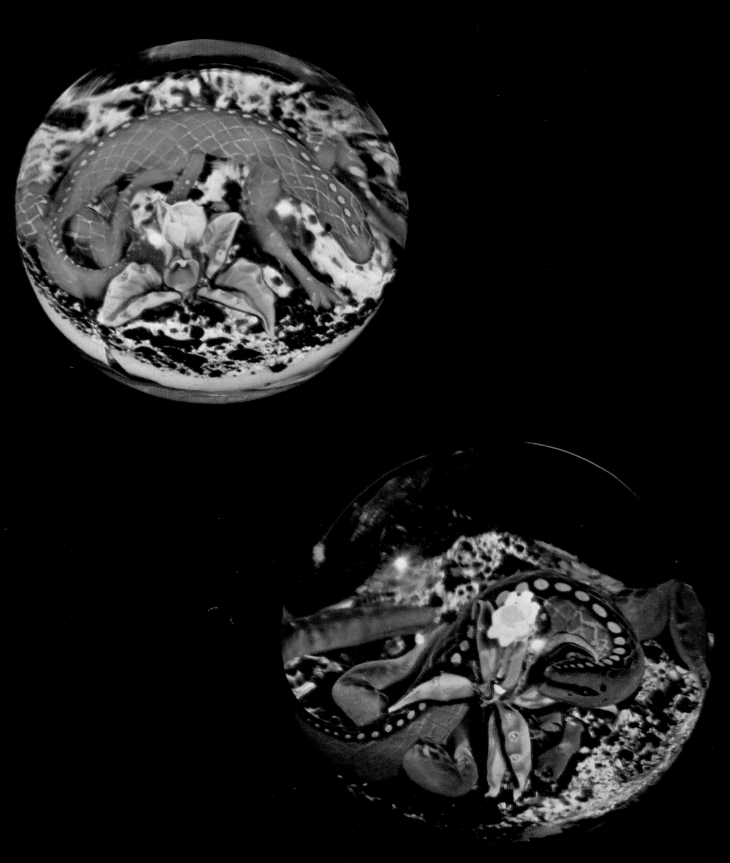

This special category includes a limited number of weights (37, 38, p. 113) in which a wafer of opaque white glass has been overlaid with glass of another color (red or blue) and then cut back to the white in cameo technique to produce a picture. The use of this technique in these weights of the Classic Period derived from contemporaneous glass engravings of horses in various attitudes by such Bohemian glass artists as Karl Pfohl and Friedrich Egermann. No. 245 (p. 113) is a weight with a five-ply overlay plaque in red and green with alternating layers of white, which has been intaglio cut with leaves and berries. To complete the illusion the weight itself was overlaid and faceted.

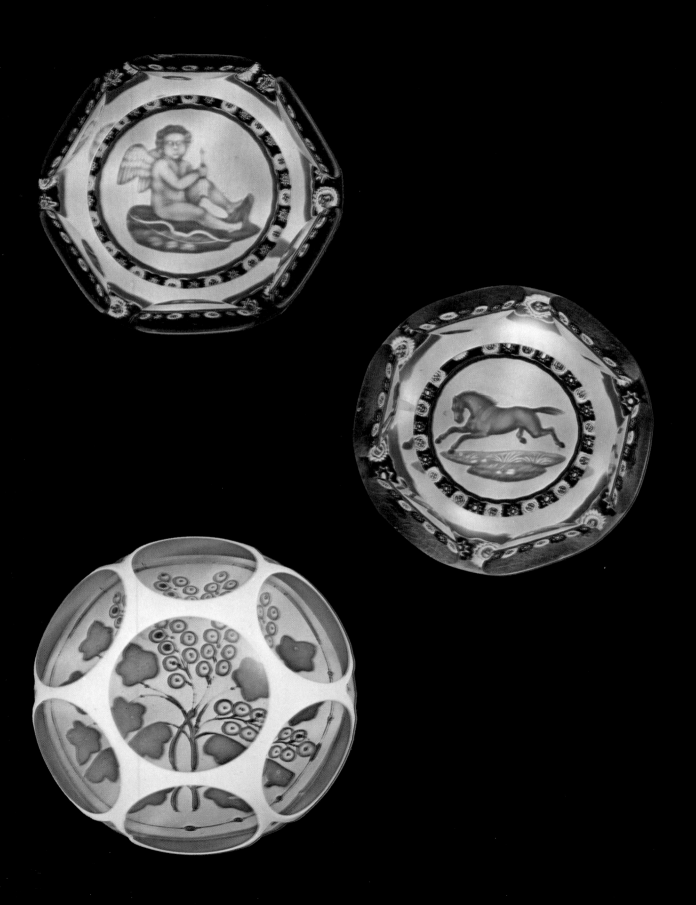

Sulphide is the name given to a glass-clay paste cameo, and also to the paperweight that encloses it. These cameos were developed in the late eighteenth century and were, until the advent of the paperweight, used to decorate a variety of glass vessels and objects.

Weights 82, 83, 158, and 236 (p. 115) were selected for this exhibition because they show, in an astonishing variety of settings, the one constant in a period of great change—Queen Victoria herself. We see her facing right in each, and in 157 (p. 116) we see her in a rare painted sulphide together with Prince Albert, who was the guiding spirit behind the Great Exhibition and the surge of arts and industries it so conclusively represented.

The other sulphides give an idea of the best that was achieved. Yet, however elegant or comely the subject, there is a sense of the unnatural when anything other than glass is embedded in glass.

The final plates on pages 118 and 119 show a painted sulphide (301) and an enameled gold foil medal (39), two subjects that were also incrusted in pressed glass tumblers. No. 244 is a cameo glass weight, brilliantly carved on both base and overlaid crown. The cameo technique was in vogue during the last two decades of the nineteenth century, when it was applied to English and French glass known today as Art Glass.

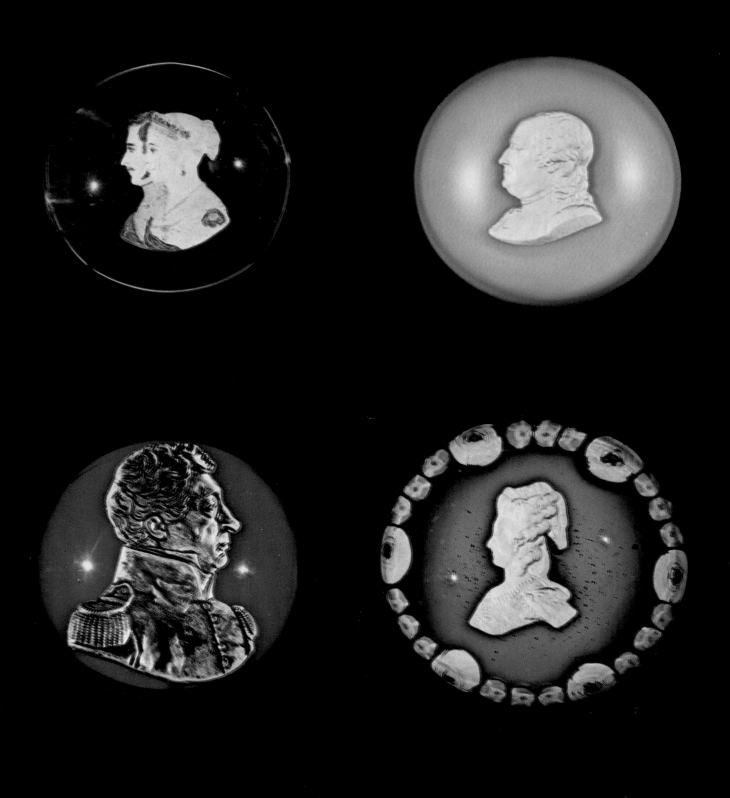

So that the subtle differences in paperweights outwardly similar but produced by different factories would be readily apparent, the examples illustrated in color in the previous section were organized by motif. In this "catalogue" section, the same weights are illustrated and described in detail. The weights are divided by country and subdivided by factory; those which proved impossible to attribute have been listed at the end. Unhappily, this "unknown" category includes some of the most interesting and impressive weights in the exhibition.

There have been many attempts to classify these "unknown" weights, with conflicting results. Paul Hollister has noted that it is essential to study both the minute details of millefiori canes and the profiles of documented weights in order to attribute paperweights accurately. The value of these techniques is undeniable, but there are numerous factories and types of weights for which there are no documented specimens. A wide variety of unusual types have been lumped under the ambiguous term "Fourth Factory," suggesting an origin other than Baccarat, Clichy, or Saint-Louis—and pointing to the factory at Pantin, France, as the likely source. Unfortunately, no weights documented to that factory have been found, so none can yet be attributed authoritatively. Further research on this factory and its products would be of great importance.

It is hoped that chemical analysis will ultimately untangle conflicting attributions. At present the cost of an analysis is still too high and the sampling method is often too destructive to be useful. Thus, until new techniques are developed to overcome these limitations, attention should be directed to other characteristics which are easier to measure or to observe. For example, tabulations by factory of the density of paperweights and the index of refraction of their covering glasses have indicated that these characteristics may be useful in attributing undocumented weights. Ultraviolet fluorescence has also been used, but with such mixed results that the technique is largely shunned today.

The fluorescence of glass is a complicated phenomenon. Essentially, fluorescence is the absorption of one color of light and the simultaneous re-emission of light of a different, longer wavelength (or color). When many colorless (and some colored) glasses are irradiated with ultraviolet light, they emit light in the visible spectrum—light which can be seen by the eye. The specific colors observed are the products of many variable factors: the ingredients in the glass, its processing, and the "color" of the ultraviolet light, to name only a few of the most significant.

If the formulas used in making the colorless encasing glass had varied from factory to factory, and if the batches had been reasonably controlled (repeated) within each factory, then ultraviolet fluorescence would be a valuable identification tool. In order to assess whether either was the case, a "controlled" examination of a series of signed weights was conducted using a single ultraviolet lamp.* The results were encouraging—so much so that nearly every weight in this catalogue (and many more that are not) were tested. Selected, signed weights were always used as reference "color standards."

Unfortunately, it is still not possible to define precisely the fluorescence "characteristics" of weights from any factory; the tests conducted are too limited in their scope for any definitive pronouncements. As noted, *only signed specimens* from Baccarat, Clichy, and Saint-Louis were used and these necessarily included only millefiori types. There are no known signed lampworked weights from these factories and only Baccarat weights are dated over a reasonably long period (1846-1858). Saint-Louis weights are dated from 1845 to 1849 and only those dated 1848 were available for this test; there are no known Clichy weights with date-canes. Nonetheless, the following fluorescence colors were observed *consistently*: a cloudy, pale pink in Baccarat weights, a much brighter, coral-pink for Saint-Louis, and a pale, lime-green for Clichy.

These results are promising, but they beg the question of whether different glass formulas could have been used in making millefiori weights. However, the great majority of non-millefiori weights *conventionally* attributed to these three factories exhibit the same fluorescence characteristics as their signed "cousins." A few do not. The former are listed

*Blak-Ray, model B-100A, long-wave (3660A) ultraviolet lamp, manufactured by Ultra-Violet Products, Inc., San Gabriel, Calif. While it is generally advisable and useful to observe both the long- and short-wave fluorescence of glass, the short-wave fluorescence of paperweights from Baccarat, Clichy and Saint-Louis, examined so far, is visually indistinguishable. The short-wave fluorescence of the weights in this catalogue has not, therefore, been reported.

in this catalogue alongside the signed specimens, but the attributions of the latter are more questionable, and in the few cases where there has been no agreement as to manufacturer in the published references and where the fluorescence does not match any of the documented groups, the weight has been given the designation "unknown factory" (as, for example, the famous salamander weights, Nos. 278-286). In a few instances, weights which had been relegated previously to the "unknown" category, but exhibited fluorescences matching those of signed weights, have been grouped with the latter (for example, the "ducks in the pond" weights, Nos. 78-80, are listed under Baccarat here, and the hollow weights which enclose lampworked roses, Nos. 202-204, are now listed with Saint-Louis weights); the attribution of one famous weight has been changed outright (the lily-of-the-valley weight, No. 201, formerly attributed to Clichy is assigned to Saint-Louis).

There is little doubt that there are weights labeled "unknown" which were actually made by the three factories mentioned—and it is likely that there are weights attributed to these factories which were not made by them. The former is especially likely with weights made by Baccarat, Clichy, and Saint-Louis after the 1845-1855 decade (after 1858 in the case of Baccarat), which are impossible to attribute so far. (To understand why, one need only note that the fluorescence of the documented 1867 weight from Saint-Louis, No. 238, is of a color entirely different from those dated 1848.) Likewise, there is still no apparent way to sort out the discrepancies in fluorescence of either American or English weights due to the scarcity of signed or documented specimens. The situation is paralleled by the weights from the other late nineteenth-century European factories. There has been no attempt in this catalogue to edit or to change long-held attributions in those areas.

The attributions given here are scaled from "signed" or "documented," to "attributed," "probably," and, at the lowest level of confidence, "possibly." The latter term is used to identify weights which *may* have been made by the factory specified, but for which there is conflicting evidence.

DPL

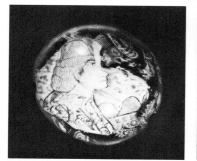

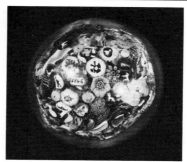

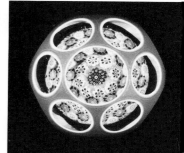

**1. Italy, Venice, Murano (attrib.), ca. early sixteenth century**

Spherical ball pierced with a cylindrical hole, enclosing scattered millefiori canes, gold foil, and an irregularly-shaped opaque white plaque enameled with a portrait of a young man with pale yellow curly hair, wearing a brick-red cap, dressed in a brick-red decorated tunic; green, blue, and yellow hills and mottled blue sky in the background.

D. 5.0 cm (1 31/32 in.)
Private collection
Fluorescence: yellow-green
Color illustration, page 26

*The portrait "plaque" was probably broken from an enameled lattimo object and then encased along with the millefiori canes.*

**2. Italy, Pietro Bigaglia (signed), Venice (Murano), dated 1845**

Scrambled millefiori canes and short lengths of filigree twists, including animal and gondola silhouettes; one cane inscribed "POB/1845."

D. 7.2 cm (2 13/16 in.)
The Hon. and Mrs. Amory Houghton, Sr., Corning, New York
Fluorescence: cloudy lime-green
Color illustration, page 26

*Bigaglia exhibited paperweights at the Exhibition of Austrian Industry in Vienna in 1845.*

**3. Italy, Pietro Bigaglia (attrib.), Venice (Murano), dated 1846**

Scrambled millefiori canes and short lengths of filigree twists, including a variety of animal silhouettes; a ribbed pink cane with a dark blue silhouette of a double-headed eagle, inscribed "FI" on its breast, and a pink-ribbed cane inscribed "1846."

D. 7.7 cm (3 1/32 in.)
Private collection
Fluorescence: cloudy yellow-green
Color illustration, page 26

*Formerly owned by the Austrian Emperor Ferdinand I and presented by him to the Austrian Emperor Franz Josef in 1848.*

**4. Europe, Bohemia (attrib.), ca. 1845-55**

Spaced concentric rings of millefiori canes, the outer row with eight pink roses, alternating with white and blue canes; above a background of scrambled lengths of filigree twists; double overlay (red over white), with large, circular windows on the sides and top of the weight.

D. 7.4 cm (2 7/8 in.)
The Art Institute of Chicago, (gift of Arthur Rubloff, No. 223)
Fluorescence: cloudy, yellowish
Color illustration, page 30

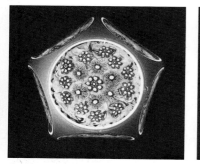

**5. Europe, Bohemia (attrib.), ca. 1845-55**

Red, white, and green millefiori canes arranged in concentric rings on a red and white filigree ground; double overlay, cut with circular windows on the sides and on the top; the bottom star-cut.

D. 7.1 cm (2¾ in.)
Private collection
Fluorescence: cloudy, yellowish
Color illustration, page 30

*"Filigree" is the term used for rods incorporating lace-like twists, usually opaque white; this term has been substituted for the designations, "muslin," "upset muslin," etc., which describe the ground in this weight. In the past this weight has been attributed to the Gillinder and Gilliland factories.*

**6. Europe, Bohemia (attrib.), ca. 1845-55**

Basket with white stave sides and red and white twist rim, base, and loop handle, the rounded top with three concentric rings of canes; the bottom of the weight star-cut.

D. 6.9 cm (2 23/32 in.)
Private collection
Fluorescence: cloudy, yellow-green; four canes at the center fluoresce a brilliant yellow-green
Color illustration, page 42

**7. Europe, Bohemia (attrib.), ca. 1845-55**

Basket with white stave sides and olive-green rim and base; red and yellow twisted handle; the rounded top of the basket holds four rings of canes; circular facets on the sides of the weight and on the top; cut panels with rounded tops at the base; the bottom star-cut.

D. 7.7 cm (3 1/32 in.)
Mr. and Mrs. Alan E. Symonds
Fluorescence: cloudy yellow-green; the rim of the basket fluoresces a brilliant yellow-green
Color illustration, page 42

**8. Europe, Bohemia (attrib.), ca 1845-55**

"Crown" weight of white filigree twists, each enclosing either a blue, pink, or white twist; with a pink and white silhouette cane cluster at the top, center.

D. 6.2 cm (2 7/16 in.)
The John Nelson Bergstrom Art Center and Museum, Neenah, Wisconsin (No. 468)
Fluorescence: brilliant yellow-green
Color illustration, page 56

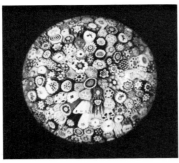

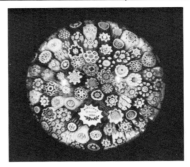

**Compagnie des Cristalleries de Baccarat, Baccarat, France**
**Founded 1764; operating today**

**Documented nineteenth-century paperweights and by-products: signed weights and other objects, dated from 1846 to 1858.**

**9. France, Baccarat (attrib.), dated 1853; made by Martin Kayser**
Close millefiori, including one cane inscribed "1853"; acid-etched mark on the bottom, "Baccarat/France" in a circle, with a decanter and two glasses.

D. 7.8 cm (3¹/₁₆ in.)
Municipality of Baccarat, France, courtesy of Mr. André Vulliet, Baccarat, Inc.
Fluorescence: cloudy, pale pink; several canes fluoresce a brilliant yellow-green
Color illustration, page 27

*Discovered in the ruins of the church in Baccarat after World War II; it is the only known Baccarat weight dated 1853. The acid-etched mark was added after its discovery.*

**10. France, Baccarat (signed), dated 1858**
Close millefiori, including one ribbed blue and white cane inscribed "BACCARAT/21 AVRIL/1858."

D. 7.2 cm (2²⁷/₃₂ in.)
The Corning Museum of Glass (No. 55.3.116; gift of the Hon. Amory Houghton, Sr.)
Fluorescence: cloudy, pale pink; several canes fluoresce a brilliant yellow-green
Color illustration, page 27

*One of several weights made to commemorate the visit of Maréchel Canrobert to Baccarat.*

**11. France, Baccarat (attrib.), ca. 1845-55**
Triple weight, the lower part with close millefiori; the central part with spaced canes, including silhouettes arranged in a circle on a filigree ground; the miniature top with an upright blue flower and foliage.

H. 8.2 cm (3⁷/₃₂ in.)
The Corning Museum of Glass (No. 66.3.48)
Fluorescence: cloudy, pale pink; several yellow canes fluoresce a brilliant yellow-green
Color illustration, page 30

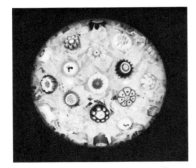

**12. France, Baccarat (attrib.), ca. 1845-55**
Spaced millefiori canes arranged in concentric circles with a pink rose cane at the center, on a filigree ground.

D. 7.4 cm (2¹⁵/₁₆ in.)
The Art Institute of Chicago (gift of Arthur Rubloff, No. 83)
Fluorescence: cloudy, pale pink; several canes fluoresce a brilliant yellow-green
Color illustration, page 30

**13. France, Baccarat (attrib.), ca. 1845-55**
"Handcooler" with spaced millefiori canes, including silhouettes, above a filigree ground; decorated with gilded star ornaments.

D. 5.1 cm (2¹/₁₆ in.); L. 6.8 cm (2¹¹/₁₆ in.)
The Corning Museum of Glass (No. 55.3.141; gift of the Hon. Amory Houghton, Sr.)
Fluorescence: cloudy, pale pink; several canes fluoresce a brilliant yellow-green
Color illustration, page 30

*Ovoid, egg-shaped objects are usually referred to as "handcoolers." It is generally theorized that since they were a convenient size to be held, ladies used them to cool their hands.*

**14. France, Baccarat (attrib.), ca. 1845-55**
A circle of six large cog-shaped canes around a central cane, above a filigree ground.

D. 8.0 cm (3⅛ in.)
The Art Institute of Chicago (gift of Arthur Rubloff, No. 87)
Fluorescence: cloudy, pale pink; several cane centers fluoresce a brilliant yellow-green
Color illustration, page 30

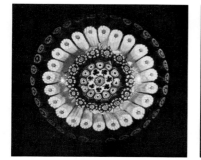

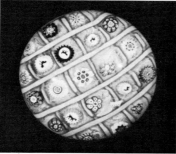

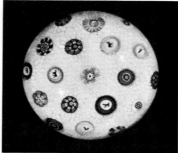

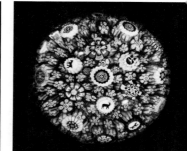

**15. France, Baccarat (attrib.), ca. 1845-55**
Spaced, concentric circles of millefiori rods, with a cluster of green shamrocks near the center; encircled by spaced rings of ribbed canes, arrowhead canes, star canes, and ribbed canes; on a white filigree ground.

D. 8.1 cm (3³/₁₆ in.)
The Hon. and Mrs. Amory Houghton, Sr., Corning, New York
Fluorescence: cloudy, pale pink
Color illustration, page 38

**16. France, Baccarat (attrib.), dated 1849**
Spaced millefiori canes, including silhouettes and one "1849" cane, arranged in a checkerboard pattern by overlapping lengths of transparent turquoise blue-clad opaque white rods, above a filigree ground.

D. 8.2 cm (3⁷/₃₂ in.)
The Illinois State Museum, Springfield (No. 702332; Morton D. Barker collection)
Fluorescence: cloudy, pale pink; several canes fluoresce a brilliant yellow-green
Color illustration, page 39

*Generally termed a "checker" weight.*

**17. France, Baccarat (signed), dated 1848**
"Carpet" of white star canes, inset with three concentric circles of spaced canes, including silhouettes and one inscribed "B/1848."

D. 7.8 cm (3⅛ in.)
The Corning Museum of Glass (No. 55.3.121; gift of the Hon. Amory Houghton, Sr.)
Fluorescence: cloudy, pale pink; two canes fluoresce a brilliant yellow-green
Color illustration, page 31

**18. France, Baccarat (signed), dated 1848**
A loose "carpet" of red millefiori canes with blue and white centers; inset with spaced concentric circles of canes, including silhouettes and one inscribed "B/1848."

D. 7.8 cm (3⅛ in.)
The Hon. and Mrs. Amory Houghton, Sr., Corning, New York
Fluorescence: cloudy, pale pink; two canes fluoresce brilliant yellow-green
Color illustration, page 32

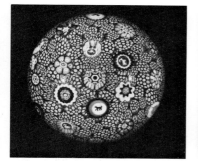

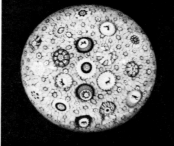

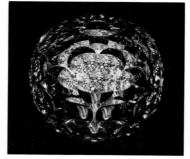

**19. France, Baccarat (signed), dated 1848**
"Carpet" of blue and white millefiori canes with concentric circles of spaced canes, including silhouettes and one inscribed "B/1848."

D. 7.8 cm (3¹/₁₆ in.)
The Art Institute of Chicago (gift of Arthur Rubloff, No. 614)
Fluorescence: cloudy, pale pink; one cane fluoresces a brilliant yellow-green
Color illustration, page 32

**20. France, Baccarat (signed), dated 1848**
"Carpet" of aqua honeycomb canes with red and white ribbed centers; inset with concentric circles of spaced canes, including silhouettes and one inscribed "B/1848."

D. 7.9 cm (3³/₃₂ in.)
The Illinois State Museum, Springfield (No. 702298; Morton D. Barker collection)
Fluorescence: cloudy, pale pink; several canes fluoresce a brilliant yellow-green
Color illustration, page 32

**21. France, Baccarat (attrib.), ca. 1845-55**
Mushroom of close millefiori; the weight with rings of circular facets on the sides, and a large circular facet on the top; the base star-cut.

D. 14.9 cm (5⅞ in.)
The Illinois State Museum, Springfield (No. 702344; Morton D. Barker collection)
Fluorescence: cloudy, pale pink; several canes fluoresce a brilliant yellow-green.
Color illustration, page 44

*Weights with diameters greater than 3½ inches are generally called magnums. Although paperweights were apparently sold by size, there is no evidence that manufacturers considered 3½ inches a significant size.*

**22. France, Baccarat (attrib.), ca. 1845-55**
Mushroom of white star clusters, with an arrowhead cane at the center; encircled by a spiral *torsade* at the base; the bottom of the weight star-cut.

D. 8.2 cm (3¼ in.)
The John Nelson Bergstrom Art Center and Museum, Neenah, Wisconsin (No. 508)
Fluorescence: cloudy, pale pink
Color illustration, page 46

*So-called "Bouquet de marriage" weight. Note that torsades on Baccarat weights spiral to the left, whereas those used by Saint-Louis spiral to the right.*

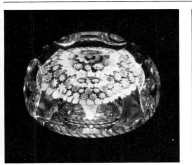

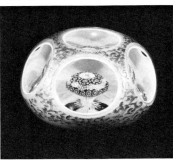

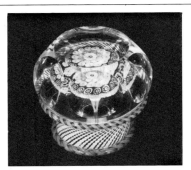

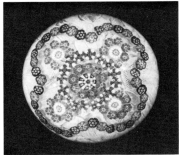

**23. France, Baccarat (attrib.), ca. 1845-50**
Mushroom with four concentric rings of canes, one with roses, around a central ruffled cane; the sides sheathed with white staves; encircled by a spiral *torsade* at the base; circular facets on the sides and on the top of the weight; the bottom star-cut.
D. 7.3 cm (2⅞ in.)
Private collection
Fluorescence: cloudy, pale pink; several canes fluoresce a brilliant yellow-green
Color illustration, page 46

**24. France, Baccarat (attrib.), ca. 1845-55**
Small mushroom with concentric rings of millefiori canes, the inner with arrowhead canes, around a star cluster; opaque white and translucent turquoise blue double overlay; five cut circular windows on the sides of the weight and one on the top, decorated with gilded scrolls; the bottom star-cut.
D. 8.0 cm (3³/₁₆ in.)
The John Nelson Bergstrom Art Center and Museum, Neenah, Wisconsin (No. 1157; gift of Mrs. Florence Gosselin Marsh in memory of her husband, Raymond Clark Marsh)
Fluorescence: cloudy, pale pink
Color illustration, page 46

**25. France, Baccarat (attrib.), ca. 1845-55**
Mushroom with four concentric rings of canes encircling a star center; six circular facets cut on the sides of the weight and one on the top; set on a hollow, waisted basket with threaded sides and *torsade* rim and foot.
D. 8.2 cm (3⁷/₃₂ in.); OH. 7.7 cm (3¹/₃₂ in.)
Louis Lyons, New York
Fluorescence: cloudy, pale pink; the yellow threads in the basket fluoresce a brilliant yellow-green
Color illustration, page 43
*There are only two known Baccarat pedestal weights; the other is in The Art Institute of Chicago.*

**26. France, Baccarat (attrib.), ca. 1845-55**
Quatrefoil garland of alternating pink and green canes, around loops of blue canes; concentric rings of blue and red-white-and-green canes, with a central arrowhead cane; on a filigree ground.
D. 7.6 cm (3 in.)
Illinois State Museum, Springfield (No. 702403; gift of Morton D. Barker)
Fluorescence: cloudy, pale pink
Color illustration, page 51

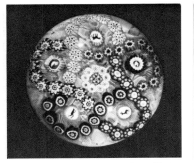

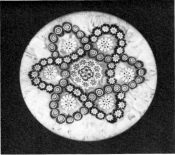

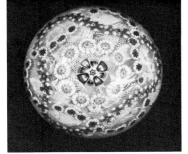

**27. France, Baccarat (attrib.), ca. 1845-55**
Interlocking cinquefoil of millefiori canes, each loop of a different color, enclosing silhouette canes in the loops, and a ring of star canes and an arrowhead cane at the center; on a white filigree ground.
D. 8.6 cm (3⅜ in.)
Private collection
Fluorescence: cloudy, pale pink; several canes fluoresce a brilliant yellow-green
Color illustration, page 49

**28. France, Baccarat (attrib.), ca. 1845-55**
Two interlaced trefoil garlands of green and red canes, with yellow shamrock canes in each loop; a ring of canes at the center, encircling an arrowhead cane; on a filigree ground.
D. 8.3 cm (3¼ in.)
The Art Institute of Chicago (gift of Arthur Rubloff, No. 575)
Fluorescence: cloudy, pale pink; several canes fluoresce a brilliant yellow-green
Color illustration, page 49

**29. France, Baccarat (attrib.), ca. 1845-55**
Two interlaced trefoil garlands of canes; a ring of pink-and-white canes encircling an arrowhead cane at the center; over a filigree ground.
D. 7.9 cm (3⅛ in.)
Private collection
Fluorescence: cloudy, pale pink
Color illustration, page 50

**30. France, Baccarat (attrib.), ca. 1845-55**
"Carpet" of white star canes, with an inset quatrefoil garland of blue canes; a red star cane in each lobe, and a red, white, and blue cane cluster at the center.
D. 7.9 cm (3³/₃₂ in.)
Private collection, courtesy of Spink & Son, Ltd., London
Fluorescence: cloudy, pale pink
Color illustration, page 49

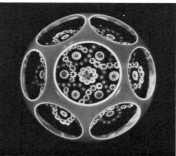

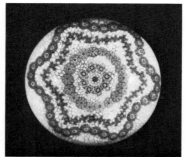

**31. France, Baccarat (attrib.), ca. 1845-55**
Two interlaced trefoil garlands of canes, with a large cane at the center and large canes in each lobe of the garlands; white "stardust ground."

D. 8.0 cm (3⅛ in.)
Private collection
Fluorescence: cloudy, pale pink
Color illustration, page 50

**32. France, Baccarat (attrib.), ca. 1845-55**
Two interlaced trefoil garlands of blue and white canes, enclosing star and arrowhead canes in the lobes; a ring of star canes and an arrowhead cane at the center; opaque white and translucent red double overlay, with cut circular and oval windows on the sides and a circular window on the top of the weight.

D. 8.1 cm (3³/₁₆ in.)
The John Nelson Bergstrom Art Center and Museum, Neenah, Wisconsin (No. 568)
Fluorescence: cloudy, pale pink
Color illustration, page 50

**33. France, Baccarat (attrib.), ca. 1845-55**
Two concentric rings of green and vermilion canes and two six-lobed stars of red and blue canes in a white "stardust ground."

D. 7.5 cm (2³¹/₃₂ in.)
Dr. and Mrs. Daniel S. Turner, New York
Fluorescence: cloudy, pale pink
Color illustration, page 50

**34. France, Baccarat (attrib.), ca. 1845-55**
Six-loop garland of red canes, with blue and white canes in the outer lobes and green canes in the inner; a ring of blue canes around an arrowhead cane at the center; white filigree ground.

D. 7.8 cm (3¹/₁₆ in.)
The Art Institute of Chicago (gift of Arthur Rubloff, No. 551)
Fluorescence: cloudy, pale pink
Color illustration, page 49

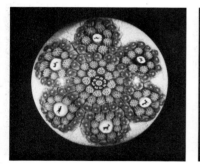

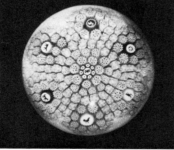

**35. France, Baccarat (attrib.), ca. 1845-55**
Paneled carpet of white star canes, with inset circular blue panels, each enclosing rings of shamrock canes and silhouettes; two rings of shamrock canes at the center, enclosing an arrowhead cane.

D. 7.9 cm (3⅛ in.)
Private collection, courtesy of Spink & Son, Ltd., London
Fluorescence: cloudy, pale pink; several canes fluoresce a brilliant yellow-green
Color illustration, page 33

**36. France, Baccarat (attrib.), ca. 1845-55**
Circular medallions of red and yellow shamrock canes encircling silhouettes, in a carpet of orange, green, and yellow whorls; bordered with a carpet of red-centered white "stardust" canes.

D. 7.8 cm (3¹/₁₆ in.)
Mr. and Mrs. Alan E. Symonds
Fluorescence: cloudy, pale pink; several canes fluoresce a brilliant yellow-green
Color illustration, page 33

**37. France, Baccarat (attrib.), ca. 1845-55**
Encased circular overlay plaque, blue on white, decorated with an engraved running horse; encircled with a ring of alternating red and white canes; six large circular facets on the sides of the weight and one on the top.

D. 8.5 cm (3¹¹/₃₂ in.)
The John Nelson Bergstrom Art Center and Museum, Neenah, Wisconsin (No. 503)
Fluorescence: cloudy, pale pink
Color illustration, page 113

**38. France, Baccarat (attrib.), ca. 1845-55**
Encased circular overlay plaque, pink on white, with an engraved cupid; encircled with a ring of green and white canes; six circular cut facets on the sides of the weight and one on the top.

D. 8.3 cm (3¼ in.)
Private collection, courtesy of Alan Tillman (Antiques) Ltd., London
Fluorescence: cloudy, pale pink
Color illustration, page 113

**39. France, Baccarat (attrib.), ca. 1845-55**
Simulated medal of the Legion of Honor, of enameled gold, encircled by a ring of canes; the sides of the weight cut with diamond-shaped facets; the top with a flat facet; the bottom of the weight star-cut.

D. 7.4 cm (2⅞ in.)
The Corning Museum of Glass (No. 55.3.67; gift of the Hon. Amory Houghton, Sr.)
Fluorescence: cloudy, pale pink
Color illustration, page 119

**40. France, Baccarat (attrib.), ca. 1845-55**
Purple, blue, and white pansy with yellow center, encircled by a ring of arrowhead canes; on a filigree ground.

D. 8.1 cm (3³/₁₆ in.)
Private collection, courtesy of Spink & Son, Ltd., London
Fluorescence: cloudy, pale pink; the center cane fluoresces a brilliant yellow-green
Color illustration, page 70

**41. France, possibly Baccarat, ca. 1845-55**
A flower with five blue petals; yellow, black, and green center; pointed green sepals, green stem and leaves.

D. 6.5 cm (2⁹/₁₆ in.)
Private collection
Fluorescence: cloudy, pale pink
Color illustration, page 70

*The flower has often been termed a "dog rose" or "pelargonium." The fluorescence of this weight is consistent with Baccarat weights, not Saint-Louis (to which it has been attributed in the past). Similar flowers seem to have been made by both factories.*

**42. France, Baccarat (attrib.), ca. 1845-55**
Primrose with five red deeply cupped petals and cream-colored star honeycomb cane center, green stem and leaves; the bottom of the weight star-cut.

D. 6.4 cm (2¹⁷/₃₂ in.)
Dr. and Mrs. Daniel S. Turner, New York
Fluorescence: cloudy, pale pink
Color illustration, page 64

**43. France, Baccarat (attrib.), ca. 1845-55**
Primrose with five white-lined, cupped pink petals and star cane center; green stem and leaves; the bottom of the weight star-cut.

D. 6.9 cm (2²³/₃₂ in.)
Private collection
Fluorescence: cloudy, pale pink
Color illustration, page 64

**44. France, Baccarat (attrib.), ca. 1845-55**
Primrose with five pink-lined, cupped white petals; star honeycomb center; green stem and leaves; the bottom of the weight star-cut.

D. 5.1 cm (2 in.)
Private collection
Fluorescence: cloudy, pale pink; the center cane fluoresces a brilliant yellow-green
Color illustration, page 64

*Collectors usually refer to weights whose diameters are less than two inches as "miniatures." There is no evidence that the factories ever made such a distinction.*

**45. France, Baccarat (attrib.), ca. 1845-55**
Primrose with yellow-lined, white cupped petals and star cane at the center; green stem and leaves; the bottom of the weight star-cut.

D. 7.7 cm (3 in.)
Mr. and Mrs. Paul Jokelson, New York, New York
Fluorescence: cloudy, pale pink; the yellow petals fluoresce a brilliant yellow-green
Color illustration, page 64

**46. France, Baccarat (attrib.), ca. 1845-55**
Primrose with five red and yellow petals and with a star center cane; green stem and leaves; encircled by a ring of alternating star and arrowhead canes; the bottom of the weight star-cut.

D. 5.0 cm (2 in.)
Mr. and Mrs. Franklin Schuell, South Bend, Indiana
Fluorescence: cloudy, pale pink; the yellow petals fluoresce a brilliant yellow-green
Color illustration, page 63

**47. France, Baccarat (attrib.), ca. 1845-55**
Primrose with six lavender, blue, and white petals and star center cane; green stem and leaves.

D. 7.8 cm (3¹/₁₆ in.)
Dr. and Mrs. Daniel S. Turner, New York
Fluorescence: cloudy, pale pink
Color illustration, page 63

**48. France, Baccarat (attrib.), ca. 1845-55**
Flower with mauve-striped and yellow petals, a star cane at the center; green stem, leaves, and a yellow bud; the bottom of the weight star-cut.

D. 8.0 cm (3⁵/₃₂ in.)
Private collection
Fluorescence: cloudy, pale pink
Color illustration, page 63

**49. France, Baccarat (attrib.), ca. 1845-55**
Primrose with six yellow, red, and opalescent pink loop-banded petals, and star cane at the center; green stem and leaves, and a green and white bud.

D. 7.6 cm (3 in.)
Private collection
Fluorescence: cloudy, pale pink; the yellow bands fluoresce a brilliant yellow-green
Color illustration, page 63

**50. France, Baccarat (attrib.), ca. 1845-55**
Daisy with overlapping, ribbed white petals, with honeycomb star center cane; green stem and leaves, and a green and white bud; cut circular facets on the sides of the weight and one on the top; the bottom star-cut.

D. 8.1 cm (3³/₁₆ in.)
The Art Institute of Chicago (gift of Arthur Rubloff, No. 299)
Fluorescence: cloudy, pale pink; the center fluoresces a brilliant yellow-green in part
Color illustration, page 65

**51. France, Baccarat (attrib.), ca. 1845-55**
Wheatflower with overlapping, ribbed, and blue-speckled white petals, and honeycomb star center cane; green stem and leaves.

D. 7.5 cm (2¹⁵/₁₆ in.)
Private collection
Fluorescence: cloudy, pale pink; the center cane fluoresces a brilliant yellow-green
Color illustration, page 65

*A similar wheatflower was included in a sheet of designs from Baccarat.*

**52. France, possibly Baccarat, ca. 1845-55**
Yellow clematis flower and two buds; green stem and leaves; six cut circular facets on the sides of the weight and one on the top; the bottom star-cut.

D. 5.0 cm (2 in.)
Mr. and Mrs. Franklin Schuell, South Bend, Indiana
Fluorescence: cloudy, pale blue
Color illustration, page 66

*Weights with similar flowers and buds share this "non-Baccarat" fluorescence; they have been attributed to Baccarat in the past, but the construction of the lampworked elements is different from that in other flower weights which exhibit a "typical" Baccarat fluorescence.*

**53. France, Baccarat (attrib.), ca. 1845-55**
Two clematis-like flowers, one double, with overlapping petals; the petals pink-striped on the upper surface and blue-striped on the underside; blue and white center canes; green stems and leaves; the bottom of the weight star-cut.

D. 7.1 cm (2¹³/₁₆ in.)
Private collection
Fluorescence: cloudy, pale pink
Color illustration, page 65

**54. France, Baccarat (attrib.), ca. 1845-55**
Large dahlia with several layers of overlapping ribbed "plush" red petals and a star cane center; green leaves and stem; the bottom of the weight star-cut.

D. 8.0 cm (3⅛ in.)
The Art Institute of Chicago (gift of Arthur Rubloff, No. 180)
Fluorescence: cloudy, pale pink
Color illustration, page 67

*The same flower is illustrated in a Baccarat design sheet.*

**55. France, Baccarat (attrib.), ca. 1845-55**

Naturalistic dark red, multi-petaled rose, with green stem and ribbed leaves.

D. 7.1 cm (2$^{13}$/$_{16}$ in.)
Private collection
Fluorescence: cloudy, pale pink
Color illustration, page 81

*So-called "1000-petal" rose. A similar rose was included in a sheet of designs from Baccarat.*

**56. France, Baccarat (attrib.), ca. 1845-55**

Pale salmon "pompon" of multi-petaled, circular form; with yellow star cane center; green stem and leaves, and two vermilion and pale green striped buds; encircled by a ring of alternating green and white canes; six large circular facets cut on the sides of the weight; the bottom star-cut.

D. 8.4 cm (3$^{5}$/$_{16}$ in.)
The John Nelson Bergstrom Art Center and Museum, Neenah, Wisconsin (No. 224)
Fluorescence: cloudy, pale pink; the yellow center cane fluoresces a brilliant yellow-green
Color illustration, page 69

**57. France, Baccarat (attrib.), ca. 1845-55**

Mottled pink and blue "pompon" of multi-petaled circular form with yellow cane center; green stem and green leaves, and a red and green bud; encircled by a ring of canes; the bottom of the weight star-cut.

D. 6.5 cm (2$^{9}$/$_{16}$ in.)
The Art Institute of Chicago (gift of Arthur Rubloff, No. 505)
Fluorescence: cloudy, pale pink; the center cane fluoresces a brilliant yellow-green
Color illustration, page 69

**58. France, Baccarat (attrib.), ca. 1845-55**

Orange Crown Imperial, with three, three-petaled flowers; green stems and leaves.

D. 7.4 cm (2$^{24}$/$_{32}$ in.)
The John Nelson Bergstrom Art Center and Museum, Neenah, Wisconsin (No. 870; given in honor of Mrs. Hugh R. Moore)
Fluorescence: cloudy, lavender-pink
Color illustration, page 71

**59. France, Baccarat (attrib.), ca. 1845-55**

Three fringed gentians, the ribbed pink blossoms lined with white; green stem and leaves, and a pink bud; the bottom of the weight star-cut.

D. 7.8 cm (3$^{1}$/$_{16}$ in.)
Private collection
Fluorescence: cloudy, pale pink
Color illustration, page 71

**60. France, Baccarat (attrib.), ca. 1845-55**

Flat bouquet of flowers, with a circular blue "pompon" at the center, flanked by two pansies, a daisy, and a bud; entwined green stems and leaves; the bottom of the weight star-cut.

D. 8.7 cm (3$^{7}$/$_{16}$ in.)
Mr. and Mrs. Alan E. Symonds
Fluorescence: cloudy, pale pink; the center canes fluoresce a brilliant yellow-green
Color illustration, page 75

**61. France, Baccarat (attrib.) ca. 1845-55**

A cross-shaped bouquet of five circular, multi-petaled "pompons," two dark red and two white flowers on the ends, one yellow flower at the center; green stems, leaves, and four buds (two red and two white); circular facets cut on the sides of the weight and one on the top; the bottom of the weight star-cut.

D. 9.1 cm (3$^{9}$/$_{16}$ in.)
The Corning Museum of Glass (No. 55.3.84; gift of the Hon. Amory Houghton, Sr.)
Fluorescence: cloudy, pale pink; the central flower fluoresces a brilliant yellow-green
Color illustration, page 75

**62. France, Baccarat (attrib.), ca. 1845-55**

Four clematis blossoms, two blue and two white, with overlapping ribbed petals and cane centers; with crossed green stems and leaves, one blue and green bud; the bottom of the weight star-cut.

D. 7.7 cm (3$^{1}$/$_{16}$ in.)
Private collection
Fluorescence: cloudy, pale pink
Color illustration, page 75

**63. France, Baccarat (attrib.), ca. 1845-55**
Flat bouquet of flowers with a ribbed, white clematis blossom, three small ribbed blue flowers, and a red and white primrose; green stems and leaves; the bottom of the weight star-cut.

D. 7.6 cm (2³¹/₃₂ in.)
Private collection
Fluorescence: cloudy, pale pink
Color illustration, page 76

**64. France, Baccarat (attrib.), ca. 1845-55**
Flat bouquet with pink, multi-petaled rose, a blue and white primrose, a purple and yellow pansy, and a black-speckled yellow wheatflower; crossed green stems and leaves and red and blue buds.

D. 8.1 cm (3³/₁₆ in.)
The Art Institute of Chicago (gift of Arthur Rubloff, No. 95)
Fluorescence: cloudy pale pink; the yellow flowers fluoresce a brilliant yellow-green
Color illustration, page 75

**65. France, Baccarat (attrib.), ca. 1845-55**
Flat floral spray, with two crossed green branches of flowers, one with ribbed, small white bellflowers, and the other with tiny red-centered white flowers, both with white buds and green leaves; six circular facets cut on the sides of the weight and one on the top; the bottom star-cut.

D. 6.7 cm (2⁵/₈ in.)
The Art Institute of Chicago (gift of Arthur Rubloff, No. 480)
Fluorescence: cloudy, pale pink
Color illustration, page 77

**66. France, Baccarat (attrib.), ca. 1845-55**
Floral bouquet with six blossoms, including both pink and blue clematis, a pink buttercup, a blue and white primrose, and a flower formed of sections of canes; two buds, intertwined green stems and leaves; six circular facets cut on the sides of the weight and one on the top; the bottom star-cut.

D. 9.1 cm (3⁹/₁₆ in.)
Mary Rich De Waters, Staten Island, New York
Fluorescence: cloudy, pale pink
Color illustration, page 75

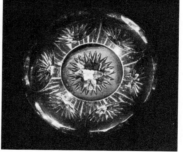

**67. France, Baccarat (attrib.), ca. 1845-55**
Upright bouquet of flowers and foliage; with circular facets cut on the top and sides of the weight.

D. 12.0 cm (4¹¹/₁₆ in.)
Illinois State Museum, Springfield (No. 702402; gift of Morton D. Barker)
Fluorescence: cloudy, pale pink
Color illustration, page 87

**68. France, Baccarat (attrib.), ca. 1845-55**
"Handcooler" containing an upright bouquet of flowers and foliage; the ovoid form with cut triangular faceting.

D. 5.1 cm (2 in.); H. 6.7 cm (2⁵/₈ in.)
Mr. and Mrs. Franklin Schuell, South Bend, Indiana
Fluorescence: cloudy, pale pink
Color illustration, page 87

**69. France, Baccarat (attrib.), ca. 1845-55**
Small upright bouquet of flowers and foliage; the weight encased with a transparent ruby overlay, with circular windows cut on the sides and top of the weight, and rounded flutes at the base; the bottom star-cut.

D. 8.3 cm (3¼ in.)
Private collection, courtesy of Spink & Son, Ltd., London
Fluorescence: cloudy, pale pink
Color illustration, page 88

**70. France, Baccarat (attrib.), ca. 1845-55**
Upright bouquet of flowers and foliage; encircled by a spiral red *torsade* at the base; circular facets cut on the sides of the weight; the bottom star-cut.

D. 8.2 cm (3¼ in.)
Dr. and Mrs. Daniel S. Turner, New York
Fluorescence: cloudy, pale pink
Color illustration, page 88

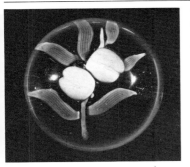

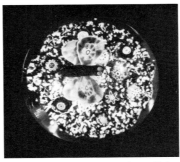

**71. France, possibly Baccarat, ca. 1845-55**
Two realistic apricots on a green branch, with ribbed green leaves.
D. 7.0 cm (2¾ in.)
The John Nelson Bergstrom Art Center and Museum, Neenah, Wisconsin (No. 815)
Fluorescence: ashy, pale pink
Color illustration, page 95
*The fluorescence of this unique weight is similar to, but not exactly the same as that usually found in Baccarat weights.*

**72. France, Baccarat (attrib.), ca. 1845-55**
Three strawberries, two ripe red and one green, with green foliage; the bottom of the weight star-cut.
D. 7.5 cm (2¹⁵/₁₆ in.)
The Corning Museum of Glass (No. 55.3.103; gift of the Hon. Amory Houghton, Sr.)
Fluorescence: cloudy, pale pink
Color illustration, page 95

**73. France, Baccarat (attrib.), ca. 1845-55**
Small butterfly with purple-coated filigree body and mottled wings made from cane slices, hovering over a green and white "jasper" ground set with canes.
D. 8.3 cm (3¼ in.)
Mr. Nelson Gustin, Los Angeles, California
Fluorescence: cloudy, pale pink; several canes fluoresce a brilliant yellow-green
Color illustration, page 101

**74. France, Baccarat (attrib.), ca. 1845-55**
Small butterfly with purple-clad filigree body and mottled wings made from cane slices, hovering over a ribbed lavender clematis blossom with star center cane; green stem and leaves; the bottom of the weight star-cut.
D. 6.4 cm (2¹⁷/₃₂ in.)
Private collection
Fluorescence: cloudy, pale pink; portions of the wings fluoresce a brilliant yellow-green
Color illustration, page 101

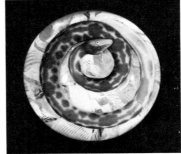

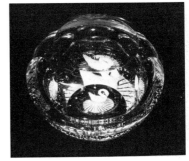

**75. France, Baccarat (attrib.), ca. 1845-55**
Two lavender bellflowers and a bud on a green branch with leaves; a butterfly profile, with purple-clad filigree body and mottled raised wings (made from cane slices) perched on the branch; six circular facets cut on the sides of the weight and one on the top; the bottom of the weight star-cut.
D. 10.0 cm (3¹⁵/₁₆ in.)
The Art Institute of Chicago (gift of Arthur Rubloff, No.74)
Fluorescence: cloudy, pale pink; parts of the wing fluoresce a brilliant yellow-green
Color illustration, page 101

**76. France, Baccarat (attrib.), ca. 1845-55**
Green filigree spiral snake, on a green and tan sandy ground.
D. 7.9 cm (3³/₃₂ in.)
The Art Institute of Chicago (gift of Arthur Rubloff, No. 485)
Fluorescence: cloudy, pale pink
Color illustration, page 105
*An apparently unique approach to portraying a snake. The filigree twists to the left, characteristic of Baccarat.*

**77. France, Baccarat (attrib.), ca. 1845-55**
Mottled green and brown spiral snake on a filigree ground.
D. 7.4 cm (2⅞ in.)
The John Nelson Bergstrom Art Center and Museum, Neenah, Wisconsin (No. 99)
Fluorescence: cloudy, pale pink
Color illustration, page 105

**78. France, possibly Baccarat, late nineteenth century**
Hollow weight, with a white swan in the air space; circular facets cut on the sides of the weight and one on the top; cut disk foot, enclosing a ring of white- and mica-flecked transparent green glass near the edge; the bottom of the weight star-cut.
D. 8.2 cm (3¼ in.)
The Hon. and Mrs. Amory Houghton, Sr., Corning, New York
Fluorescence: cloudy, pale pink
Color illustration, page 103

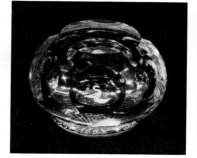

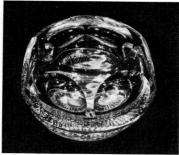

**79. France, possibly Baccarat, late nineteenth century**
Hollow weight, with a white swan and two striped ducks in the air space; cut circular facets on the sides of the weight and on the top; cut disk foot, enclosing a ring of mica-flecked, transparent green glass near the edge; the bottom of the weight star-cut.

D. 7.9 cm (3⅛ in.)
The Corning Museum of Glass (No. 64.3.81; gift of the Hon. Amory Houghton, Sr.)
Fluorescence: cloudy, pale pink; the ducks fluoresce a brilliant yellow-green
Color illustration, page 103

**80. France, possibly Baccarat, late nineteenth century**
Hollow weight, with three striped ducks in the air space; circular facets cut on the sides of the weight and one on the top; cut disk foot, enclosing a ring of white- and mica-flecked transparent green glass near the edge; the bottom of the weight star-cut.

D. 8.2 cm (3¼ in.)
The Corning Museum of Glass (No. 55.3.77; gift of the Hon. Amory Houghton, Sr.)
Fluorescence: cloudy, pale pink; the yellow stripes fluoresce a brilliant yellow-green
Color illustration, page 103

**81. France, possibly Baccarat, ca. 1845-55**
Sulphide profile portrait, on a transparent red disk base; a circular facet cut on the top of the weight, decorated with a gilded border, and encircled by a ring of gold-outlined, white enamel dots; the sides decorated with a gilded vine; the bottom of the weight star-cut.

D. 8.9 cm (3½ in.)
The John Nelson Bergstrom Art Center and Museum, Neenah, Wisconsin (No. 250)
Fluorescence: cloudy, pale pink
Color illustration, page 117

*Heretofore, the portrait has been identified as that of Charles X, but it seems more likely that it is of*

*Louis Philippe. The weight had been attributed to Bohemia, but its fluorescence and construction are the same as those in (attributed) Baccarat weights.*

**82. France, possibly Baccarat, ca. 1845-55**
Brilliant red over white, double overlay weight, with cut circular windows on the sides and top, revealing a sulphide profile portrait of the young Queen Victoria within; the bottom of the weight star-cut.

D. 9.9 cm (3⅞ in.)
The New-York Historical Society (No. 1965.465.B; bequest of Mrs. Jennie H. Sinclair)
Fluorescence: not certain; overlay affects the fluorescence of the colorless glass
Color illustration, page 115

**83. France, Baccarat (attrib.), ca. 1845-55**
Sulphide profile portrait of the young Queen Victoria, inscribed "VICTORIA I REINE DE LA GRANDE BRETAGNE" in a circle around the portrait; on a transparent red disk base; diamond-shaped facets cut on the sides of the weight and a concave facet on the top.

D. 8.6 cm (3⅜ in.)
The John Nelson Bergstrom Art Center and Museum, Neenah, Wisconsin (No. 1080; gift of Mrs. Florence Gosselin Marsh in memory of her husband, Raymond Clark Marsh)
Fluorescence: cloudy, pale pink
Color illustration, page 115

**84. France, Baccarat (attrib.), ca. 1845-55**
Sulphide portrait of Joan of Arc, shown holding a sword, with her helmet resting on a tree stump; framed with oak and laurel branches; on a transparent green ground; diamond-shaped facets cut on the sides of the weight, and flat on the top.

D. 8.8 cm (3¹⁵/₃₂ in.)
The John Nelson Bergstrom Art Center and Museum, Neenah, Wisconsin (No. 480)
Fluorescence: cloudy, pale pink
Color illustration, page 117

**85. France, Baccarat (attrib.), ca. 1845-55**
Sulphide of a hunter and dog; on a transparent blue disk base; diamond-shaped facets cut on the sides of the weight, and a concave facet on the top.

D. 8.6 cm (3⅜ in.)
The John Nelson Bergstrom Art Center and Museum, Neenah, Wisconsin (No. 216)
Fluorescence: cloudy, pale pink
Color illustration, page 117

*A similar weight, on a green ground, was given by the Baccarat factory to the Conservatoire des Arts et Métiers, Paris, in April 1851. It was described as a "Press-papiers, avec camée chasse sur fond vert, lustré à facettes."*

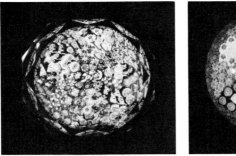

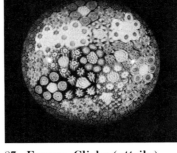

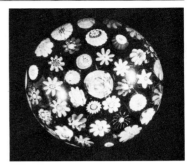

**L. J. Maës, Clichy-la-Garenne, France**
Founded ca. 1837 at Billancourt (Pont-de Sèvres), moved to Clichy-la-Garenne ca. 1839; absorbed to become part of the Cristalleries de Sèvres et Clichy in 1885

**Documented nineteenth-century paperweights and by-products: signed weights and other objects, none dated.**

**86. France, Clichy (signed), ca. 1845-55**
Close millefiori, including one cane of rods spelling "CLICHY," at the side; concave facets cut on the top and sides of the weight.

D. 8.1 cm (3³/₁₆ in.)
The Corning Museum of Glass (No. 55.3.117; gift of the Hon. Amory Houghton, Sr.)
Fluorescence: cloudy, pale lime-green; several canes fluoresce a brilliant yellow-green
Color illustration, page 26

**87. France, Clichy (attrib.), ca. 1845-55**
Closely-set medallions of millefiori canes, encircled by a ring of green star canes.

D. 8.2 cm (3³/₁₆ in.)
The Art Institute of Chicago (gift of Arthur Rubloff No. 553)
Fluorescence: cloudy, lime-green; several canes fluoresce a brilliant yellow-green
Color illustration, page 27

**88. France, Clichy (attrib.), dated 1851**
Concentric circles of spaced millefiori canes, with two large pink "Clichy roses"; the flat base inscribed with an engraved and polished crown, an intertwined block-letter monogram "V/A," and the inscription "LONDRES/1851."

D. 9.4 cm (3²³/₃₂ in.)
The Corning Museum of Glass (No. 55.3.73; gift of the Hon. Amory Houghton, Sr.)
Fluorescence: cloudy, pale lime-green
Color illustration, page 29

*Presumably exhibited at "The Great Exhibition of the Works of Industry of all Nations" (The Crystal Palace) in 1851.*

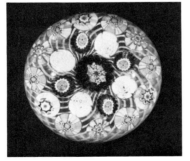

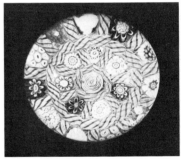

**89. France, Clichy (attrib.), ca. 1845-55**
Concentric rings of millefiori canes, including four white "Clichy roses," above a white double spiral lattice on an opaque red ground.

D. 5.4 cm (2⅛ in.)
The Art Institute of Chicago (gift of Arthur Rubloff, No. 463)
Fluorescence: cloudy, lime-green; several cane centers fluoresce a brilliant yellow-green
Color illustration, page 29

*The only recorded example of a Clichy weight with a red ground and double spiral lattice.*

**90. France, Clichy (attrib.), ca. 1845-55**
Square canes, on a white filigree ground, on a bed of parallel white spiral twists; circular facets on the sides and one on the top.

D. 7.6 cm (2³¹/₃₂ in.)
Private collection
Fluorescence: cloudy, lime-green; several canes fluoresce a brilliant yellow-green
Color illustration, page 29

*As at Saint-Louis, Clichy used filigree twists which spiral from left to right.*

**91. France, Clichy (attrib.), ca. 1845-55**
Concentric circles of spaced millefiori canes, including a pink and a white "Clichy rose"; separated by short lengths of blue and white filigree twists, above a filigree ground and backed by a bed of parallel lengths of white filigree twists.

D. 7.9 cm (3³/₃₂ in.)
Private collection
Fluorescence: cloudy, lime-green
Color illustration, page 39

*A so-called "checker" weight.*

**92. France, Clichy (attrib.), ca. 1845-55**
Newel post finial, containing spaced millefiori canes, including a pink "Clichy rose" at the center, separated by short lengths of white filigree twists, above a bed of parallel lengths of white filigree twists; cut vertical facets at the base of the ball; ground cylindrical shank.

D. 9.3 cm (3⅝ in.); OH. 13.3 cm (5¼ in.)
Private collection
Fluorescence: cloudy, lime-green
Color illustration, page 39

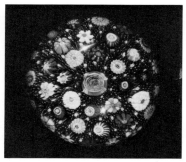

**93. France, Clichy (signed), ca. 1845-55**
Spaced millefiori canes, with a large pink "Clichy rose" at the center, in a green "moss" ground; one cane of rods spelling the word "CLICHY" on the underside of the ground, behind the rose.

D. 8.2 cm (3¼ in.)
G. E. Carter
Fluorescence: not tested
Color illustration, page 32

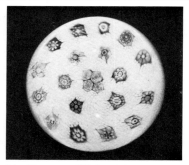

**94. France, Clichy (signed), ca. 1845-55**
Concentric circles of spaced millefiori canes, with four small pink "Clichy roses" at the center, one cane inscribed "C" at the side, set in a white "stardust carpet" ground; in a blue and white stave "basket."

D. 5.6 cm (2⁷/₃₂ in.)
Private collection
Fluorescence: cloudy, lime-green; several canes fluoresce a brilliant yellow-green
Color illustration, page 31

**95. France, Clichy (attrib.), ca. 1845-55**
Concentric circles of spaced millefiori cane clusters, set into a white "stardust carpet" ground; about a central pink "Clichy rose"; in a green and white stave "basket."

D. 6.4 cm (2½ in.)
Private collection
Fluorescence: cloudy, lime-green; several canes fluoresce a brilliant yellow-green
Color illustration, page 31

**96. France, Clichy (attrib.), ca. 1845-55**
Two spaced rings of millefiori canes encircling a pink "Clichy rose."

D. 4.5 cm (1¹³/₃₂ in.)
Mr. and Mrs. Franklin Schuell, South Bend, Indiana
Fluorescence: cloudy, lime-green
Color illustration, page 38

**97. France, Clichy (attrib.), ca. 1845-55**
Concentric rings of millefiori canes, the outer row with five pink and green "Clichy roses"; about a central red and white star; opaque brilliant blue ground.

D. 4.2 cm (1⅝ in.)
Illinois State Museum, Springfield (No. 702369; gift of Morton D. Barker)
Fluorescence: cloudy, lime-green
Color illustration, page 38

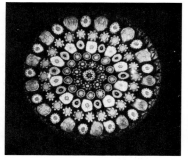

**98. France, Clichy (attrib.), ca. 1845-55**
Concentric rings of millefiori canes, the next-to-the-outer row containing thirteen "Clichy roses"; in a transparent light blue and opaque white stave "basket."

D. 8.3 cm (3¼ in.)
The New-York Historical Society (No. 1965.491.C; bequest of Mrs. Jennie H. Sinclair)
Fluorescence: cloudy, lime-green
Color illustration, page 38

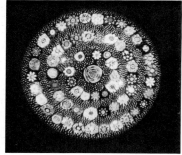

**99. France, Clichy (attrib.), ca 1845-55**
Concentric rings of millefiori canes, including both pink and white "Clichy roses," alternating with rings of green "moss" canes; a pink "Clichy rose" at the center; alternating blue and white stave sides.

D. 7.4 cm (2¹⁵/₁₆ in.)
Private collection
Fluorescence: cloudy, lime-green
Color illustration, page 37

**100. France, Clichy (attrib.), ca. 1845 (dated)**
Pedestal weight with domed top, containing concentric rings of canes, the next-to-the-outer with thirteen white "Clichy roses," and the next with twenty-one similar pink and green roses, with a similar pink and green rose at the center; blue and white stave sides; gilded metal foot, decorated with stylized flowers on the top, an engraved inscription, "ESCALIER DE CRISTAL 1845," on the bottom.

D. 7.5 cm (2³¹/₃₂ in.)
Illinois State Museum, Springfield (No.702323; gift of Morton D. Barker)

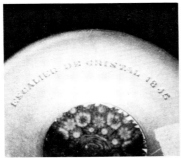

Photograph of base of 100.

Fluorescence: cloudy, lime-green; several canes fluoresce a brilliant yellow-green
Color illustration, page 43

*The Escalier de Cristal was a shop in the Palais Royale in Paris. This is the only known Clichy weight datable to 1845.*

**101. France, Clichy (signed), ca. 1845-55**
Pedestal weight with domed top, containing rings of polychrome canes alternating with concentric rings of white "stardust" canes with blue centers; the outer row made up of green "moss" canes; a pink and green "Clichy rose" at the center and one cane inscribed "C"; blue and white spiral stave sides; disk foot (replaced).

D. 6.0 cm (2⅜ in.)
Mr. and Mrs. Paul Jokelson, New York, New York
Fluorescence: cloudy, lime-green
Color illustration, page 43

**102. France, Clichy (signed), ca. 1845-55**
Mushroom with close millefiori canes, one inscribed "C"; pink and white stave sides; opaque white and translucent pink overlay, with four large circular windows and small ovals cut on the sides and one circular window on the top of the weight; the bottom star-cut.

D. 7.0 cm (2¾ in.)
Private collection
Fluorescence: cloudy, lime-green
Color illustration, page 45

**103. France, Clichy (attrib.), ca. 1845-55**
Mushroom with millefiori canes and alternating green and white stave sides; the weight with opaque white overlay cut into vertical stripes, with cut flutes between; a pink and green "Clichy rose" cane on the surface on the top.

D. 7.1 cm (2¹³/₁₆ in.)
Private collection
Fluorescence: cloudy, lime-green
Color illustration, page 45

**104. France, Clichy (attrib.), ca. 1845-55**
Mushroom with white stave sides, the top with concentric rings of canes, the outer of green "moss" canes, and the next with eleven pink "Clichy roses," around a similar large rose at the center; six circular facets cut on the sides of the weight and one on the top; the bottom star- and petal-cut.

D. 8.6 cm (3⅜ in.)
The John Nelson Bergstrom Art Center and Museum, Neenah, Wisconsin (No. 504)
Fluorescence: cloudy, lime-green
Color illustration, page 47

**105. France, Clichy (attrib.), ca. 1845-55**
Mushroom with alternating pink and white stave sides, the top with concentric rings of canes, the fourth with eleven white "Clichy roses," around a similar central pink rose; translucent white overlay, with five large circular windows cut on the sides of the weight and one on the top; crosshatched cutting on the bottom.

D. 7.8 cm (3¹/₁₆ in.)
The New-York Historical Society (No. 1965.481.C; bequest of Mrs. Jennie H. Sinclair)
Fluorescence: cloudy, lime-green
Color illustration, page 47

**106. France, Clichy (attrib.), ca. 1845-55**
Mushroom with white stave sides and concentric rings of canes, the second with alternating red-and-white and purple "Clichy roses," around a similar pink rose at the center; opaque white and translucent dark green double overlay, cut circular windows on the sides of the weight and on the top; crosshatched cutting on the bottom.

D. 8.0 cm (3⅛ in.)
The John Nelson Bergstrom Art Center and Museum, Neenah, Wisconsin (No. 505)
Fluorescence: cloudy, lime-green; several canes fluoresce a brilliant yellow-green
Color illustration, page 47

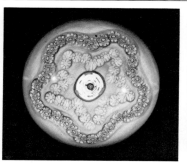

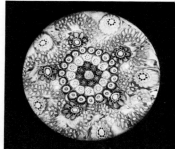

**107. France, Clichy (attrib.),
ca. 1845-55**
Mushroom with alternating white
and blue stave sides, and concentric rings of canes, the next to the
inner ring with five yellow "Clichy
roses," around a similar central
pink rose; white and translucent
blue double overlay, with five cut
circular windows on the sides of
the weight and one on the top;
cross-hatched cutting on the
bottom.

D. 8.2 cm (3⁷/₃₂ in.)
The Hon. and Mrs. Amory
Houghton, Sr., Corning, New York
Fluorescence: cloudy, lime-green
Color illustration, page 47

**108. France, Clichy (attrib.),
ca. 1845-55**
Carpet of hexagonal bands of
millefiori canes.

D. 7.9 cm (3⅛ in.)
Private collection
Fluorescence: cloudy, lime-green;
several canes fluoresce a brilliant
yellow-green
Color illustration, page 36

**109. France, Clichy (attrib.),
ca. 1845-55**
Two five-pointed garlands of canes,
with a central white and red
"Clichy rose"; on a brilliant red
ground

D. 6.8 cm (2⅝ in.)
Private collection
Fluorescence: cloudy, lime-green
Color illustration, page 50

**110. France, Clichy (attrib.),
ca. 1845-55**
Five-looped garland of turquoise
blue canes, enclosing green canes
in the lobes, and concentric rings
encircling a pink "Clichy rose";
pink canes outside the lobes; on a
filigree ground, backed by a bed of
parallel lengths of opaque white
filigree twists.

D. 8.2 cm (3¼ in.)
Illinois State Museum, Springfield
(No. 702324; gift of Morton
D. Barker)
Fluorescence: cloudy, lime-green
Color illustration, page 52

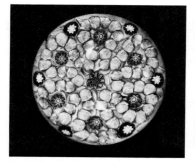

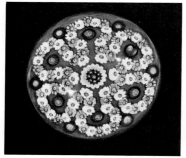

**111. France, Clichy (attrib.),
ca. 1845-55**
Six-looped garland of pink and
green "Clichy roses," with brilliant
blue canes in the lobes, dark red
canes outside, and a ruffled green
cane at the center; on a filigree
ground.

D. 7.8 cm (3¹/₁₆ in.)
Private collection
Fluorescence: cloudy, lime-green
Color illustration, page 52

*The number of rose canes in this
weight—66—is, apparently, the
"record."*

**112. France, Clichy (attrib.),
ca. 1845-55**
Six-looped garland of pale blue
canes, with deep burgundy canes
inside each lobe, and pink canes
outside; a pink "Clichy rose" at the
center; on a filigree ground;
backed by a bed of parallel lengths
of white filigree twists.

D. 7.9 cm (3⅛ in.)
Private collection
Fluorescence: cloudy, lime-green
Color illustration, page 52

**113. France, Clichy (attrib.),
ca. 1845-55**
Six-looped garland of alternating
pink and white ruffled canes, with
green canes in the lobes, blue
canes outside, and a cane cluster
at the center; on a brilliant blue
ground.

D. 8.3 cm (3¼ in.)
The Corning Museum of Glass
(No. 56.3.110; gift of the Hon.
Amory Houghton, Sr.)
Fluorescence: cloudy, lime-green
Color illustration, page 53

**114. France, Clichy (attrib.),
ca. 1845-55**
Six C-scrolls and three concentric
rings of canes, one of pink "Clichy
roses"; on a brilliant blue ground.

D. 7.7 cm (3¹/₃₂ in.)
The Hon. and Mrs. Amory
Houghton, Sr., Corning, New York
Fluorescence: cloudy, lime-green
Color illustration, page 53

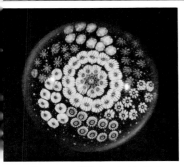

**115. France, Clichy (attrib.), ca. 1845-55**
Six looped garlands of canes, two of pink and white "Clichy roses," around concentric rings of canes and a pink cane at the center; set into a green "moss" ground.
D. 7.8 cm (3 1/32 in.)
Batiste, London
Fluorescence: cloudy, lime-green
Color illustration, page 53

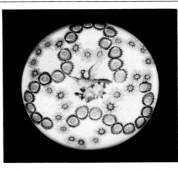

**116. France, Clichy (attrib.), ca. 1845-55**
Two interlaced trefoil garlands of pink and green canes, with an enameled gold foil plaque at the center with a bird and flowers; on a white ground.
D. 7.9 cm (3 1/8 in.)
Mr. and Mrs. Paul Jokelson, New York, New York
Fluorescence: cloudy, lime-green
Color illustration, page 51

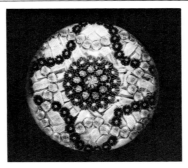

**117. France, Clichy (attrib.), ca. 1845-55**
Two interlaced quatrefoil garlands, one of purple canes, the other of pink "Clichy roses"; concentric rings of green and red canes at the center, encircling a turquoise blue cane; on a filigree ground, backed with a bed of parallel white filigree twist rods.
D. 8.2 cm (3 1/4 in.)
Private collection
Fluorescence: cloudy, lime-green
Color illustration, page 52

**118. France, Clichy (attrib.), ca. 1845-55**
Two interlaced quatrefoil garlands of purple and pink canes, enclosing two concentric rings of canes and a pink "Clichy rose" in the center; set into a green "moss" ground.
D. 8.3 cm (3 1/4 in.)
The John Nelson Bergstrom Art Center and Museum, Neenah, Wisconsin (No. 486)
Fluorescence: cloudy, lime-green
Color illustration, page 52

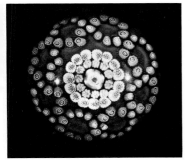

**119. France, Clichy (attrib.), ca. 1845-55**
Two interlaced quatrefoil garlands of pink and purple canes, enclosing concentric rings and a central white and green "Clichy rose"; on a dark green ground.
D. 8.0 cm (3 3/16 in.)
The Hon. and Mrs. Amory Houghton, Sr., Corning, New York
Fluorescence: cloudy, lime-green; the centers of several canes fluoresce a brilliant yellow-green
Color illustration, page 51

**120. France, Clichy (attrib.), ca. 1845-55**
Basket with white stave sides and red-and-white *torsade* rim and foot; the domed top with three concentric circles of millefiori canes (two with pink "Clichy roses"), alternating with rings of green "moss" canes; encircled by a green "moss" band with rosettes of millefiori canes (one of pink and one of white "Clichy roses"); handle missing.
H. 6.4 cm (2 1/2 in.); W. 10.9 cm (4 1/4 in.); Depth 9.9 cm (3 7/8 in.)
Dr. and Mrs. Junius T. Langston, Plainfield, New Jersey
Fluorescence: cloudy, lime-green
Color illustration, page 41

**121. France, Clichy (attrib.), ca. 1845-55**
Swirled stripes, alternately green and white, with a pink "Clichy rose" at the center.
D. 6.4 cm (2 7/32 in.)
Private collection
Fluorescence: cloudy, lime-green
Color illustration, page 55

**122. France, Clichy (attrib.), ca. 1845-55**
Swirled stripes, alternately dark blue and white, centered with a pink "Clichy rose."
D. 8.1 cm (3 3/16 in.)
Private collection
Fluorescence: cloudy, lime-green
Color illustration, page 55

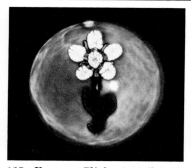

**123. France, Clichy (attrib.), ca. 1845-55**
Swirled stripes, alternately pink and white, with a blue and white star cane cluster at the center; encircled by a white filigree twist at the edge of the weight.

D. 7.9 cm (3⅛ in.)
Heritage Plantation of Sandwich, Sandwich, Massachusetts
Fluorescence: cloudy, lime-green
Color illustration, page 55

**124. France, Clichy (attrib.), ca. 1845-55**
Large, multi-petaled pink rose, made from a "Clichy rose" cane; coiled green stem and ribbed leaves; the bottom of the weight star- and petal-cut.

D. 5.1 cm (2 in.)
Mr. and Mrs. Franklin Schuell, South Bend, Indiana
Fluorescence: cloudy, lime-green
Color illustration, page 61

**125. France, Clichy (attrib.), ca. 1845-55**
A five-petaled white flower, petals and center formed of white star canes; green stem and leaves; on a vermilion ground.

D. 7.1 cm (2¹³/₁₆ in.)
Private collection
Fluorescence: cloudy, lime-green
Color illustration, page 62

**126. France, Clichy (attrib.), ca. 1845-55**
A five-petaled, white flower with blue and white cane center and green sepals; striped green stem and leaves on a brilliant blue ground.

D. 6.9 cm (2¹¹/₁₆ in.)
Private collection
Fluorescence: cloudy, lime-green
Color illustration, page 62

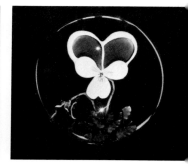

**127. France, Clichy (attrib.), ca. 1845-55**
A double flower with ribbed pink petals and a blue and white star cane at the center; with green stem and leaves on a green "moss" ground.

D. 7.2 cm (2¹³/₁₆ in.)
Private collection
Fluorescence: cloudy, lime-green
Color illustration, page 62

**128. France, Clichy (attrib.), ca. 1845-55**
A flower with pink- and lavender-striped petals and star cane center; ribbed yellow leaves and straight green stem; on a filigree ground, with a bed of parallel lengths of white filigree rods beneath.

D. 7.0 cm (2¾ in.)
The Art Institute of Chicago (gift of Arthur Rubloff, No. 809)
Fluorescence: cloudy, lime-green
Color illustration, page 62

**129. France, Clichy (attrib.), ca. 1845-55**
An exotic flower with a crown of white-tipped purple petals and yellow-tipped green stamens; cane center; green stem and leaves on a double-spiral white lattice ground.

D. 7.4 cm (2¹⁵/₁₆ in.)
Private collection
Fluorescence: cloudy, lime-green
Color illustration, page 62

**130. France, Clichy (attrib.), ca. 1845-55**
Large yellow and purple viola and bud, with green stems and leaves.

D. 7.3 cm (2⅞ in.)
Private collection
Fluorescence: cloudy, lime-green
Color illustration, page 70

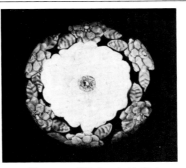

**131. France, Clichy (attrib.), ca. 1845-55**

Yellow and lavender viola and bud, with green stems and leaves, encircled by a ring of canes, with pink and green "Clichy roses" alternating with sets of star canes.

D. 6.7 cm (2⅝ in.)
Private collection
Fluorescence: cloudy, lime-green
Color illustration, page 70

**132. France, possibly Clichy, ca. 1845-55**

Pink and yellow, multi-petaled, domed, circular camellia with green leaves.

D. 8.1 cm (3³/₁₆ in.)
Private collection
Fluorescence: cloudy, gray-tan
Color illustration, page 68

*The attribution of this handsome weight to Clichy is doubtful, but its construction is closely related to others whose fluorescence is similar to that of documented weights from that factory (see no. 133).*

**133. France, Clichy (attrib.), ca. 1845-55**

Large, multi-petaled white camellia with yellow center; encircled by a ring of alternating pink and yellow flowers, each with veined green leaves.

D. 8.0 cm (3⁵/₃₂ in.)
Dr. and Mrs. Daniel S. Turner, New York
Fluorescence: cloudy, lime-green
Color illustration, page 68

**134. France, possibly Clichy, ca. 1845-55**

Large pink and red multi-petaled camellia with waffled petals and yellow center; veined green leaves.

D. 5.1 cm (2 in.)
Mr. and Mrs. Franklin Schuell, South Bend, Indiana
Fluorescence: cloudy, pale yellowish (unlike "typical" Clichy fluorescence)
Color illustration, page 68

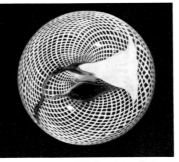

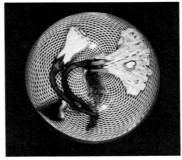

**135. France, possibly Clichy, ca. 1845-55**

Large, yellow camellia with waffled petals and yellow and green center; veined green leaves; circular facets cut on the sides of the weight and one on the top.

D. 5.2 cm (2¹/₁₆ in.)
Mr. and Mrs. Franklin Schuell, South Bend, Indiana
Fluorescence: cloudy, pale yellow (unlike "typical" Clichy fluorescence)
Color illustration, page 68

*See also no. 134.*

**136. France, Clichy (attrib.), ca. 1845-55**

Ribbed yellow morning glory with white lining, on a curving green stem, with a pointed leaf; on a double spiral white lattice ground.

D. 7.4 cm (2⅞ in.)
Private collection
Fluorescence: cloudy, lime-green
Color illustration, page 73

**137. France, Clichy (attrib.), ca. 1845-55**

Variegated blue morning glory and bud on green stems, with two heart-shaped leaves; on a double spiral white lattice ground.

D. 9.2 cm (3⁵/₈ in.)
Illinois State Museum, Springfield (No. 702405; gift of Morton D. Barker)
Fluorescence: cloudy, lime-green
Color illustration, page 73

*The bud and blossom are formed of millefiori canes.*

**138. France, Clichy (attrib.), ca. 1845-55**

Two morning glory blossoms and buds, one blue with a white lining, the other white, with a ruffled pink edge; green stems and leaves; the bottom of the weight star-cut.

D. 7.7 cm (3 in.)
Private collection
Fluorescence: cloudy, lime-green
Color illustration, page 73

**139. France, Clichy (attrib.), ca. 1845-55**
A large flower with striped pink and white petals, formed of canes split lengthwise; with a cane at the center and green and yellow stamens; with a pink bud, green stems, and ribbed green leaves.

D. 7.6 cm (3 in.)
Illinois State Museum, Springfield (No. 702471; gift of Morton D. Barker)
Fluorescence: cloudy, lime-green
Color illustration, page 72

**140. France, Clichy (attrib.), ca. 1845-55**
Three flowers and two opening buds, with striped petals formed of canes split lengthwise; cane centers; green leaves and stems.

D. 7.6 cm (3 in.)
The New-York Historical Society (No. 1965.389.C; bequest of Mrs. Jennie H. Sinclair)
Fluorescence: cloudy, lime-green
Color illustration, page 72

**141. France, Clichy (attrib.), ca. 1845-55**
Bouquet with two flowers and two buds, the petals formed of pink-and-white, lavender, and red canes; on long, straight, pink and green stems, with green leaves.

D. 7.5 cm (2³¹/₃₂ in.)
The John Nelson Bergstrom Art Center and Museum, Neenah, Wisconsin (No. 1028; gift of Mrs. Florence Gosselin Marsh in memory of her husband, Raymond Clark Marsh)
Fluorescence: cloudy, lime-green
Color illustration, page 77

**142. France, Clichy (attrib.), ca. 1845-55**
Two flowers with ribbed pink and white petals, one with a yellow and blue cane center; wiggly green sepals, green stems and leaves; on a double spiral white lattice ground.

D. 7.3 cm (2⅞ in.)
The Corning Museum of Glass (No. 72.3.151; gift of Mrs. Leigh M. Battson)
Fluorescence: cloudy, lime-green
Color illustration, page 65

**143. France, Clichy (attrib.), ca. 1845-55**
Bouquet of pink-ribbed, white flowers and foliage.

D. 6.8 cm (2¹¹/₁₆ in.)
Private collection
Fluorescence: cloudy, lime-green
Color illustration, page 76

**144. France, Clichy (attrib.), ca. 1845-55**
Three flowers with striped purple, pink, and light blue petals and buds; green leaves and stems, bound with a striped pink ribbon.

D. 7.9 cm (3⅛ in.)
Private collection
Fluorescence: cloudy, lime-green
Color illustration, page 77

**145. France, Clichy (attrib.), ca. 1845-55**
Spray with two large, multi-petaled, pink "Clichy roses" and five white flowers; green stems and leaves; on a green "moss" ground.

D. 8.1 cm (3³/₁₆ in.)
Private collection
Fluorescence: cloudy, lime-green
Color illustration, page 61

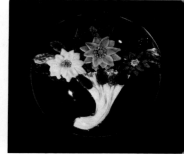

**146. France, Clichy (attrib.), ca. 1845-55**
Striped pink and white cornucopia, the closed end with a stylized head, holding three flowers, buds, and green foliage.

D. 7.8 cm (3¹/₁₆ in.)
Private collection
Fluorescence: cloudy, lime-green
Color illustration, page 76

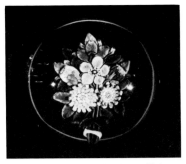

**147. France, Clichy (attrib.), ca. 1845-55**
Rectangular, opalescent white ("opaline") book-shaped plaque, with an applied oval medallion on one side, enclosing a bouquet of flowers and buds, with green leaves and stems, tied with a lavender ribbon. Crizzled.

L. 8.5 cm (3⁵/₁₆ in.); W. 5.8 cm (2⁹/₃₂ in.); Depth 2.8 cm (1¹/₁₆ in.)
Dr. and Mrs. Daniel S. Turner, New York
Fluorescence: cloudy, lime-green; several parts fluoresce a brilliant yellow-green
Color illustration, page 76

**148. France, probably Clichy, ca. 1845-55**
Bouquet of flowers and buds, one flower formed from a pink "Clichy rose" cane; green leaves and stems, tied with a pink ribbon.

D. 7.3 cm (2⅞ in.)
Private collection, courtesy of Alan Tillman (Antiques) Ltd., London
Fluorescence: cloudy, gray-green
Color illustration, page 77

**149. France, Clichy (attrib.), ca. 1845-55**
Bouquet of flowers and buds, with green leaves and stems, tied with a white ribbon.

D. 7.1 cm (2¹³/₁₆ in.)
Mr. and Mrs. Alan E. Symonds
Fluorescence: cloudy, lime-green
Color illustration, page 77

**150. France, Clichy (attrib.), ca. 1845-55**
Bouquet of flowers and buds, a purple and yellow viola at the center, with green leaves and stems, tied with a white ribbon.

D. 7.6 cm (3 in.)
Mr. and Mrs. Alan E. Symonds
Fluorescence: cloudy, bluish lime-green
Color illustration, page 77

**151. France, Clichy (attrib.), ca. 1845-55**
Bouquet with a purple and yellow viola and two three-dimensional white and yellow flowers, with two purple buds and two white buds; green leaves and stems, tied with a pink ribbon.

D. 8.5 cm (3⅜ in.)
The John Nelson Bergstrom Art Center and Museum, Neenah, Wisconsin (No. 1181; gift of Mrs. Florence Gosselin Marsh in memory of her husband, Raymond Clark Marsh)
Fluorescence: cloudy, lime-green
Color illustration, page 85

**152. France, Clichy (attrib.), ca. 1845-55**
Small pink- and green-speckled white bird with green wings, hovering over a white gardenia with a star cane at the center; green stem and leaves; on a ground of parallel white filigree rods.

D. 7.9 cm (3³/₃₂ in.)
The Corning Museum of Glass (No. 55.3.78; gift of the Hon. Amory Houghton, Sr.)
Fluorescence: cloudy, pale lime-green
Color illustration, page 101

**153. France, Clichy (attrib.), ca. 1845-55**
Large butterfly with amber-colored, striped body; the front wings made from pink and yellow honeycomb canes, the rear wings from pink and green "Clichy rose" canes.

D. 6.7 cm (2⅝ in.)
The John Nelson Bergstrom Art Center and Museum, Neenah, Wisconsin (No. 894)
Fluorescence: cloudy, gray-green
Color illustration, page 101

**154. France, probably Clichy, ca. 1845-55**
Two realistic amber pears on a mauve branch, with green leaves; on a ground of parallel lengths of white filigree rods.

D. 9.1 cm (3⁹/₁₆ in.)
The John Nelson Bergstrom Art Center and Museum, Neenah, Wisconsin (No. 300)
Fluorescence: cloudy, gray-green
Color illustration, page 98

**155. France, Clichy (attrib.), ca. 1845-55**
Sulphide profile portrait of Benjamin Franklin, on an opaque lime-green ground.

D. 7.2 cm (2²⁷/₃₂ in.)
Mr. and Mrs. Paul Jokelson, New York, New York
Fluorescence: cloudy, lime-green
Color illustration, page 116

**156. France, Clichy (attrib.), ca. 1845-55**
Sulphide profile portrait of Marie Antoinette, encircled by a ring of white "Clichy roses"; transparent green ground.

D. 8.2 cm (3¼ in.)
The Corning Museum of Glass (No. 55.3.92; gift of the Hon. Amory Houghton, Sr.)
Fluorescence: cloudy, lime-green
Color illustration, page 116

**157. France, possibly Clichy, ca. 1845-55**
Sulphide profile portraits of Victoria and Albert, realistically colored.

D. 6.8 cm (2⅝ in.)
The Art Institute of Chicago (gift of Arthur Rubloff, No. 306)
Fluorescence: cloudy, yellowish-green (slightly stronger than typical "Clichy")
Color illustration, page 116

**158. France, Clichy (attrib.), ca. 1845-55**
Sulphide profile portrait of the young Queen Victoria, on a black (purple) ground; four large cut oval bosses on the sides of the weight, with deep vertical flutes between; cut, domed top.

D. 7.2 cm (2¹³/₁₆ in.)
The John Nelson Bergstrom Art Center and Museum, Neenah, Wisconsin (No. 362)
Fluorescence: cloudy, lime-green
Color illustration, page 115
*The same sulphide is used in no. 159.*

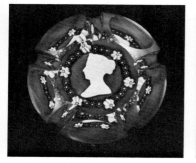

**159. France, Clichy (attrib.), ca. 1845-55**
Sulphide profile portrait of the young Queen Victoria, encircled with a ring of white canes alternating with sets of three green canes; on a brilliant red ground; five circular cut facets, with deep vertical flutes between, on the sides of the weight, and one circular facet on the top.

D. 7.2 cm (2²⁷/₃₂ in.)
The Corning Museum of Glass (No. 72.3.164; gift of Mrs. Leigh M. Battson)
Fluorescence: cloudy, lime-green
Color illustration, page 115
*See also no. 158.*

**160. France, Clichy (attrib.), ca. 1845-55**
Sulphide of a full-length statue of Napoleon Bonaparte, encircled with a ring of green canes alternating with sets of five pink canes; on a dark blue ground; five circular facets cut on the sides of the weight, and one on the top.

D. 8.6 cm (3⅜ in.)
The John Nelson Bertstrom Art Center and Museum, Neenah, Wisconsin (No. 163)
Fluorescence: cloudy, lime-green
Color illustration, page 118

**161. France, Clichy (attrib.), ca. 1845-55**
Small, circular (sulphide?) disk painted with a nautical scene at the center, encircled by six rings of canes, each enclosing a small sulphide head; six circular windows cut on the sides of the weight and one on the top

D. 8.6 cm (3⅜ in.)
Mr. and Mrs. Paul Jokelson, New York, New York
Fluorescence: cloudy, lime-green
Color illustration, page 51

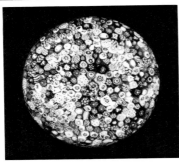

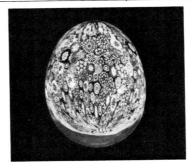

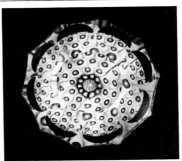

**Compagnie des Cristalleries de Saint-Louis, Saint-Louis, near Bitche, France**
Founded 1767; operating today

Documented nineteenth-century paperweights and by-products: signed weights and other objects, dated 1845 through 1849.

**162. France, Saint-Louis (attrib.), ca. 1845 (possibly earlier)**
Close millefiori, including numerous blue and white quatrefoil canes; lined with blue and white "jasper."

D. 7.6 cm. (3 in.)
The John Nelson Bergstrom Art Center and Museum, Neenah, Wisconsin (No. 439)
Fluorescence: pinkish
Color illustration, page 27

*The fluorescence of the encasing glass is difficult to see since it is so thin. A similar weight, in the Rubloff collection (The Art Institute of Chicago), is inscribed "SL."*

**163. France, Saint-Louis (attrib.), ca. 1845-55**
Ovoid "handcooler" with close millefiori.

D. 5.5 cm (2³/₁₆ in.); L. 7.4 cm (2²⁹/₃₂ in.)
The John Nelson Bergstrom Art Center and Museum, Neenah, Wisconsin (No. 205)
Fluorescence: cloudy, coral-pink
Color illustration, page 27

*Unusual in that the millefiori canes were collected in one gather; more often, two domes of millefiori canes were combined to produce "hand-coolers."*

**164. France, Saint-Louis (attrib.), ca. 1845-55**
Domed carpet of red-lined, white, ribbed canes with blue and white flower centers; a large cane cluster at the center; the sides and top of the weight cut with circular facets.

D. 7.2 cm (2²⁷/₃₂ in.)
The John Nelson Bergstrom Art Center and Museum, Neenah, Wisconsin (No. 448)
Fluorescence: cloudy, coral-pink
Color illustration, page 34

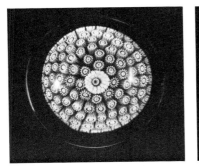

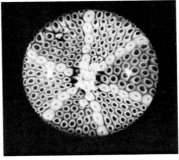

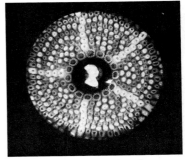

**165. France, Saint-Louis (attrib.), ca. 1845-55**
Domed carpet of green, red, and white ribbed millefiori canes, a large multiple star cane cluster at the center.

D. 7.5 cm (2¹⁵/₁₆ in.)
Private collection
Fluorescence: cloudy, coral-pink
Color illustration, page 34

**166. France, Saint-Louis (attrib.), ca. 1845-55**
Four panels of close millefiori, formed by a cross of pink and white canes, bordered with pale green and white spiral ribbons, with a blue and white cane cluster at the center.

D. 7.2 cm (2²⁷/₃₂ in.)
The New-York Historical Society (No. 1965.463.SL; bequest of Mrs. Jennie H. Sinclair)
Fluorescence: cloudy, coral-pink
Color illustration, page 35

**167. France, Saint-Louis (signed), dated 1848**
Carpet with six spokes of blue and white canes separating alternating panels of green and pink canes; a small molded sulphide pansy at the center, above an orange, blue, and white cane cluster; a cane inscribed "SL/1848" in one panel.

D. 6.3 cm (2¹⁵/₃₂ in.)
Private collection
Fluorescence: cloudy, coral-pink
Color illustration, page 35

**168. France, Saint-Louis (attrib.), ca. 1845-55**
Carpet of pink-lined, ribbed blue canes, divided into five panels by spokes of pink-lined ribbed white canes; each panel with swags and circular clusters of blue-centered, ribbed, orange-and-white canes; a sulphide portrait bust of a woman at the center, against a transparent red background, encircled with a ring of ribbed green canes.

D. 7.6 cm (2³¹/₃₂ in.)
The Art Institute of Chicago (gift of Arthur Rubloff, No. 118)
Fluorescence: cloudy, coral-pink
Color illustration, page 35

*The portrait has often been identified as Josephine, consort of Napoleon I.*

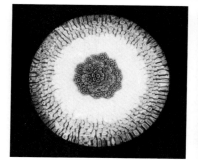

**169. France, Saint-Louis
(attrib.), ca. 1845-55**
Tricolor carpet; a circular cluster of
blue canes at the center, ringed
with concentric bands of white and
pink canes.

D. 7.1 cm (2²⁵/₃₂ in.)
The New-York Historical Society
(No. 1965.216. SL; bequest of
Mrs. Jennie H. Sinclair)
Fluorescence: cloudy, coral-pink
Color illustration, page 36

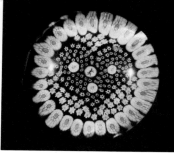

**170. France, Saint-Louis
(attrib.), ca. 1845-55**
Ring of star canes encircling a carpet of blue and white stars and a
large heart-shaped panel of red,
white, and turquoise canes, with
three white star clusters and a
devil silhouette within; the heart
outlined with red, white, and blue
stars; transparent dark green
ground.

D. 7.8 cm (3¹/₁₆ in.)
Mrs. Amory Houghton, Sr., Corn-
ing, New York
Fluorescence: cloudy, coral-pink
Color illustration, page 35

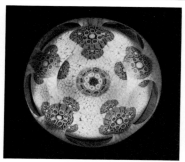

**171. France, Saint-Louis
(attrib.), ca. 1845-55**
Carpet of white "stardust" canes,
inset with six circles of red, white,
and blue cane clusters; circular
facets cut on the sides of the
weight and one on the top.

D. 8.1 cm (3³/₁₆ in.)
Private collection
Fluorescence: cloudy, coral-pink
Color illustration, page 31

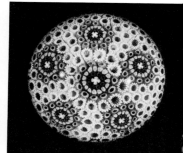

**172. France, Saint-Louis
(signed), dated 1848**
Carpet of red-lined, ribbed, white
canes, inset with six rings of red-
lined ribbed turquoise canes, each
enclosing cross-centered turquoise, blue, and white cane clusters; one cane inscribed "SL/1848"
on the side.

D. 6.6 cm (2¹⁹/₃₂ in.)
The Art Institute of Chicago (gift
of Arthur Rubloff, No. 213)
Fluorescence: cloudy, coral-pink
Color illustration, page 33

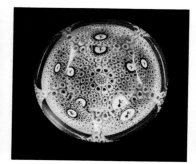

**173. France, Saint-Louis
(attrib.), ca. 1845-55**
Carpet of ribbed pink canes, inset
with six circles of ribbed pale
green canes, five enclosing
silhouette canes and one enclosing
a pink and blue cane cluster; circular facets cut on the sides of the
weight and one on the top.

D. 6.5 cm (2⁹/₁₆ in.)
The John Nelson Bergstrom Art
Center and Museum, Neenah,
Wisconsin (No. 194)
Fluorescence: cloudy, coral-pink
Color illustration, page 33

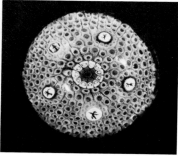

**174. France, Saint-Louis
(attrib.), ca. 1845-55**
Carpet of green-lined, ribbed,
white canes, inset with five rings
of pink-lined ribbed white canes,
each enclosing silhouette canes,
and with a cane cluster at the
center.

D. 7.3 cm (2⅞ in.)
The Corning Museum of Glass
(No. 55.3.101; gift of the Hon.
Amory Houghton, Sr.)
Fluorescence: cloudy, coral-pink
Color illustration, page 33

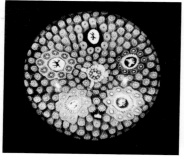

**175. France, Saint-Louis
(signed), dated 1848**
Carpet of blue star-centered,
ribbed, amber and white canes, inset with five rings of canes, each
enclosing silhouettes; with a central red, green, and white cane
cluster and four yellow spots; one
cane inscribed "SL/1848" at the
side.

D. 6.7 cm (2⅝ in.)
Private collection, courtesy of Alan
Tillman (Antiques) Ltd., London
Fluorescence: cloudy, coral-pink
Color illustration, page 33

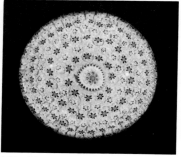

**176. France, Saint-Louis
(attrib.), ca. 1845-55**
Concentric rings of blue and white
stars alternating with rings of red
and white stars; a large ribbed red
and white cane enclosing a cane
cluster at the center; set into an
opaque yellow-green ground.

D. 8.3 cm (3¼ in.)
The Art Institute of Chicago (gift
of Arthur Rubloff, No. 43)
Fluorescence: cloudy, coral-pink
Color illustration, page 37

**177. France, Saint-Louis (attrib.), ca. 1845-55**
Nine concentric circles of millefiori canes in contrasting colors, several with tiny silhouettes of heads (possibly of Napoleon); one ring with ribbed canes enclosing floral sprigs, alternating with ribbed canes containing dog (?) silhouettes.

D. 11.1 cm (4 11/32 in.)
Illinois State Museum, Springfield (No. 702401; gift of Morton D. Barker)
Fluorescence: cloudy, coral-pink
Color illustration, page 37

**178. France, Saint-Louis (signed), dated 1848**
Pedestal weight with domed top; six concentric rings of canes encircling a cluster of red and green ribbed canes; one cane inscribed "SL/1848" in the next to outer ring; on a solid "basket" pedestal, formed of a white lattice, and with white *torsade* rim and foot.

D. 7.9 cm (3⅛ in.)
The Corning Museum of Glass (No. 55.3.68; gift of the Hon. Amory Houghton, Sr.)
Fluorescence: cloudy, coral-pink
Color illustration, page 43

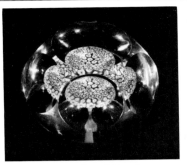

**179. France, Saint-Louis (attrib.), ca. 1845-55**
Mushroom with four concentric rings of canes, the outer ring of white canes with blue star centers; a green and red cane cluster at the center; six circular facets on the sides of the weight and one on the top; the bottom amber-stained.

D. 7.1 cm (2 13/16 in.)
The New-York Historical Society (No. 1965.214.SL; bequest of Mrs. Jennie H. Sinclair)
Fluorescence: cloudy, coral-pink
Color illustration, page 46

**180. France, Saint-Louis (attrib.), ca. 1845-55**
Mushroom with four concentric rings of canes around a central ribbed cane; encircled by a red and white spiral *torsade* at the base; six cut circular facets on the sides of the weight and one on the top; the bottom star-cut.

D. 8.3 cm (3¼ in.)
Private collection
Fluorescence: cloudy, coral-pink
Color illustration, page 46

*The torsades on Saint-Louis weights twist to the right, the reverse of the direction found in Baccarat weights.*

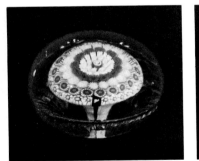

**181. France, Saint-Louis (signed), dated 1848**
Mushroom with four concentric rings of canes, around a white star cluster at the center; the outer ring with a cane inscribed "SL/1848"; encircled by a blue and white *torsade* at the base; the bottom of the weight star-cut.

D. 7.2 cm (2⅞ in.)
Private collection
Fluorescence: cloudy, coral-pink
Color illustration, page 46

**182. France, Saint-Louis (attrib.), ca. 1845-55**
Six looped garlands of canes, with a star cluster at the center; on an opaque greenish-yellow ground.

D. 7.7 cm (3 in.)
The New-York Historical Society (No. 1965.80.SL; bequest of Mrs. Jennie H. Sinclair)
Fluorescence: cloudy, coral-pink
Color illustration, page 53

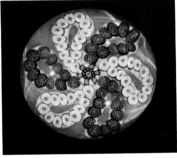

**183. France, Saint-Louis (attrib.), ca. 1845-55**
Six alternating loops of white and dark blue canes, with a cane cluster at the center; on an opaque lime-green ground.

D. 7.9 cm (3 3/32 in.)
Private collection
Fluorescence: cloudy, coral-pink
Color illustration, page 53

**184. France, Saint-Louis (attrib.), ca. 1845-55**
Hollow "crown" of pairs of red, blue, and white spiral twists (twisted in opposite directions), alternating with white filigree twists; a yellow cane cluster at the center.

D. 7.2 cm (2 27/32 in.)
The John Nelson Bergstrom Art Center and Museum, Neenah, Wisconsin (No. 390)
Fluorescence: cloudy, coral-pink
Color illustration, page 56

**185. France, Saint-Louis (attrib.), ca. 1845-55**
Hollow "crown" of red, blue, green, and white spiral twists alternating with white filigree twists; with a pink and blue cane cluster at the center.

D. 6.3 cm (2⁷/₁₆ in.)
Dr. and Mrs. Daniel S. Turner, New York
Fluorescence: cloudy, coral-pink
Color illustration, page 56

**186. France, Saint-Louis (attrib.), ca. 1845-55**
Hollow "crown" of aventurine-flecked green and gold and white spiral twists; with a pink, blue, and white cane cluster at the top.

D. 7.9 cm (3⅛ in.)
The Corning Museum of Glass (No. 63.3.35; gift of the Hon. Amory Houghton, Sr.)
Fluorescence: cloudy, coral-pink
Color illustration, page 56

**187. France, Saint-Louis, ca. 1850**
Hollow "crown" of aventurine-flecked green and gold and white spiral twists alternating with white filigree twists; centered with a blue and white cane; surmounted by a blown green pear.

D. approx. 6.4 cm (2½ in.)
Museum of the Conservatoire des Arts et Métiers, Paris
Fluorescence: not tested
Color illustration, page 99

*Given by the Saint-Louis factory to the Conservatoire des Arts et Métiers, Paris, in January 1851; called a "Presse-papiers, couronne venise, avec poire verte"—a "Venetian crown, with a green pear."*

**188. France, Saint-Louis, ca. 1847**
"Crown" newel post finial, the spherical top decorated with red, blue, and white twisted tapes, and red, green, and white tapes, alternating with white filigree twists; a cane cluster at the top; the reel-shaped stem encloses similar twists; ground, cylindrical shank, with a scalloped oval paper label on the bottom, inscribed in ink "année/1847/16."

D. 13.3 cm (5¼ in.); OH. 21.3 cm (8³/₈ in.)
Compagnie des Cristalleries de Saint-Louis, Paris
Fluorescence: cloudy, light pink
Color illustration, page 57

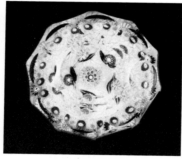

**189. France, Saint-Louis (attrib.), ca. 1845-55**
Encased opaque white dome with green and red looping; a blue and white cane cluster at the top.

D. 7.8 cm (3¹/₁₆ in.)
The John Nelson Bergstrom Art Center and Museum, Neenah, Wisconsin (No. 495)
Fluorescence: cloudy, coral-pink
Color illustration, page 55

*The type is usually termed a "marbrie" paperweight; the origin or meaning of the term is not known.*

**190. France, Saint-Louis (attrib.), ca. 1845-55**
Blue, yellow, and pink cane flowers arranged around a central pink, blue, and white cane cluster; encircled by a ring of alternating yellow and blue canes; on a filigree ground; small cut circular facets on the sides of the weight and a large circular facet on the top.

D. 6.6 cm (2⁹/₁₆ in.)
Private collection
Fluorescence: cloudy, coral-pink
Color illustration, page 60

**191. France, probably Saint-Louis, ca. 1845-55**
Flat bouquet of blue, orange, white, and pink cane flowers and green leaves, encircled by a ring of blue and white canes; small cut circular facets on the sides of the weight and one large one on the top; the bottom cross-cut with tiny diamonds, amber-stained.

D. 5.1 cm (2 in.)
Mr. and Mrs. Franklin Schuell, South Bend, Indiana
Fluorescence: cloudy pink (not "coral," as is usual for Saint-Louis; not "Baccarat" pink)
Color illustration, page 60

**192. France, Saint-Louis (attrib.), ca. 1845-55**
Floral bouquet, the flowers formed of canes, on amber stems with dark green leaves; in a pebbly, opaque white ground; encircled by a green, white, and orange spiral *torsade*; small cut circular facets on the sides and top of the weight.

D. 7.7 cm (3¹/₃₂ in.)
Private collection
Fluorescence: cloudy, coral-pink
Color illustration, page 61

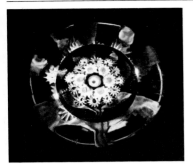

**193. France, Saint-Louis (attrib.), ca. 1845-55**
A large stemmed flower with a double ring of petals formed of canes, with green leaves; a large circular facet on the top of the weight.

D. 8.0 cm (3⅛ in.)
The Art Institute of Chicago (gift of Arthur Rubloff, No. 30)
Fluorescence: cloudy, coral-pink
Color illustration, page 61

**194. France, Saint-Louis (attrib.), ca. 1845-55**
Large dahlia with several layers of overlapping ribbed purple petals, and a yellow and red center; green aventurine leaves; star-cut base.

D. 7.4 cm (2⅞ in.)
Private collection
Fluorescence: cloudy, coral-pink
Color illustration, page 67

**195. France, Saint-Louis (attrib.), ca. 1845-55**
Large dahlia with several layers of overlapping ribbed pink petals, and an orange, blue, and white cane center; green leaves; the bottom of the weight star-cut.

D. 8.2 cm (3⁷/₃₂ in.)
Private collection
Fluorescence: cloudy, coral-pink
Color illustration, page 67

**196. France, Saint-Louis (attrib.), ca. 1845-55**
Large dahlia with several layers of overlapping pink-striped white petals; an orange, blue, and white cane at the center; green leaves; the bottom of the weight star-cut.

D. 6.4 cm (2½ in.)
The John Nelson Bergstrom Art Center and Museum, Neenah, Wisconsin (No. 560)
Fluorescence: cloudy, coral-pink
Color illustration, page 67

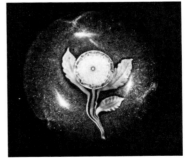

**197. France, Saint-Louis (attrib.), ca. 1845-55**
Double clematis or dahlia with overlapping pink-striped petals; a red, white, and blue cane at the center; green stem and leaves; on a double spiral white lattice ground.

D. 7.0 cm (2¾ in.)
The John Nelson Bergstrom Art Center and Museum, Neenah, Wisconsin (No. 424).
Fluorescence: cloudy, coral-pink
Color illustration, page 66

**198. France, Saint-Louis (attrib.), ca. 1845-55**
Feathery white "pompon" of multi-petaled, circular form; with small yellow cane cluster at the center; green stem and serrated green leaves, and a green and white bud; on a double spiral white and red lattice ground.

D. 7.3 cm (2⅞ in.)
The Corning Museum of Glass (No. 55.3.94; gift of the Hon. Amory Houghton, Sr.)
Fluorescence: cloudy, coral-pink
Color illustration, page 69

**199. France, Saint-Louis (attrib.), ca. 1845-55**
White "pompon" of multi-petaled, circular form; with a small yellow cane cluster at the center; green stem and veined green leaves; on a green "aventurine" ground.

D. 7.8 cm (3¹/₃₂ in.)
Private collection
Fluorescence: cloudy, coral-pink
Color illustration, page 69

**200. France, Saint-Louis (attrib.), ca. 1845-55**
White "pompon" of multi-petaled, circular form with yellow cane center; green stem and serrated green leaves; on a transparent red disk foot; five large cut circular facets on the sides of the weight and one on the top; star-cut bottom.

D. 7.9 cm (3⅛ in.)
Private collection
Fluorescence: cloudy, coral-pink
Color illustration, page 69

**201. France, Saint-Louis (attrib.), ca. 1845-55**
Spray of white lily of the valley, with white flowers and buds on a curved green stem, with green leaves; on a transparent red ground; six cut circular facets on the sides of the weight and one on the top.

D. 8.2 cm (3³/₁₆ in.)
Private collection, courtesy of Spink & Son, Ltd., London
Fluorescence: cloudy, coral-pink
Color illustration, page 71

*Although generally considered "Clichy," the fluorescence of this weight is characteristic of Saint-Louis weights; the construction of the weight is similar to no. 200.*

**202. France, probably Saint-Louis, ca. 1845-55**
Hollow weight, the air space containing a naturalistic white, multi-petaled rose, with green stem, leaves, and a green and white bud.

D. 7.9 cm (3¹/₈ in.)
The New-York Historical Society (No. 1965.357.U; bequest of Mrs. Jennie H. Sinclair)
Fluorescence: cloudy, coral-pink
Color illustration, page 80

*The attribution of weights of this type (see, also, nos. 203 and 204) is controversial. There are no documented examples, nor does their construction parallel any documented weights; their fluorescence is, however, typically "Saint-Louis."*

**203. France, probably Saint-Louis, ca. 1845-55**
Hollow weight, the air space containing a naturalistic white, multi-petaled rose, with green stem, leaves, and a white and green bud; on a translucent red and opalescent white ground; a cut circular facet on the top of the weight.

D. 7.7 cm (3¹/₁₆ in.)
The Corning Museum of Glass (No. 67.3.25; gift of the Hon. Amory Houghton, Sr.)
Fluorescence: cloudy, coral-pink
Color illustration, page 80
*See no. 202.*

**204. France, probably Saint-Louis, ca. 1845-55**
Hollow weight, the air space containing a naturalistic yellow multi-petaled rose, bud, and green stem and leaves.

D. 7.3 cm (2⁷/₈ in.)
Private collection
Fluorescence: cloudy, coral-pink
Color illustration, page 80
*See no. 202.*

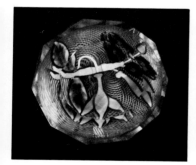

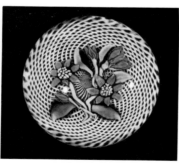

**205. France, Saint-Louis (attrib.), ca. 1845-55**
Red and blue fuchsia with two buds, on pink stems and an amber stalk, with green leaves; on a blue double swirl lattice ground; cut with flat facets on the sides and top. Re-faceted.

D. 4.6 cm (1¹³/₁₆ in.)
Private collection
Fluorescence: cloudy, coral-pink
Color illustration, page 71

**206. France, probably Saint-Louis, ca. 1845-55**
Blue flowers and buds with green and yellow centers, on green stems and leaves; double-spiral lattice ground.

D. 7.1 cm (2¹³/₁₆ in.)
The John Nelson Bergstrom Art Center and Museum, Neenah, Wisconsin (No. 137)
Fluorescence: cloudy, coral-pink
Color illustration, page 71

*Formerly attributed to the Monot, père et fils, et Stumpf factory at Pantin, but the weight's fluorescence is consistent with documented Saint-Louis weights.*

**207. France, Saint-Louis (attrib.), ca. 1845-55**
Striped green cornucopia holding a bouquet of flowers, with a ribbed blue clematis flower at the center; the bottom of the weight star-cut.

D. 7.2 cm (2¹³/₁₆ in.)
The Art Institute of Chicago (gift of Arthur Rubloff, No. 753)
Fluorescence: cloudy, coral-pink
Color illustration, page 76

**208. France, Saint-Louis (attrib.), ca. 1845-55**
Upright bouquet of flowers and foliage, a white and yellow flower at the center; encircled by a blue and white spiral *torsade* at the base; cut hexagonal faceting on the top of the weight and circular facets on the sides; the bottom of the weight star-cut.

D. 6.9 cm (2²³/₃₂ in.)
Private collection
Fluorescence: cloudy, coral-pink
Color illustration, page 88

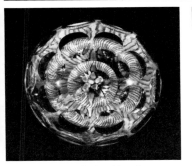

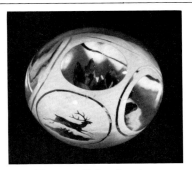

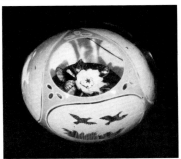

**209. France, Saint-Louis (attrib.), ca. 1845-55**
Upright bouquet of flowers and foliage; encircled by a yellow and white spiral *torsade* at the base; cut circular facets on the top and sides of the weight.

D. 7.1 cm (2¹³/₁₆ in.)
The New-York Historical Society (No. 1965.70.SL; gift of Mrs. Jennie H. Sinclair)
Fluorescence: cloudy, coral-pink
Color illustration, page 88

**210. France, probably, Saint-Louis, ca. 1845-55**
Upright bouquet of flowers and foliage; white and translucent red double overlay, with cut circular windows on the top and sides of the weight, the bottom of the weight star-cut.

D. 8.1 cm (3³/₁₆ in.)
The New-York Historical Society (No. 1965.454.SL; gift of Mrs. Jennie H. Sinclair)
Fluorescence: cloudy, pink (not coral, but the overlay may influence the color)
Color illustration, page 88

**211. France, Saint-Louis (attrib.), ca. 1845-55**
Encased white overlay, with two interior oval windows on the sides and one on the top, and two engraved oval panels, one with the silhouette of a running stag; the other with the silhouette of a running dog; revealing an upright bouquet of flowers and foliage, a blue flower at the top; the bottom of the weight star-cut.

D. 7.7 cm (3 in.)
The Corning Museum of Glass (No. 55.3.110; gift of the Hon. Amory Houghton, Sr.)
Fluorescence: cloudy, coral-pink
Color illustration, page 89

**212. France, Saint-Louis (attrib.), ca. 1845-55**
Encased double overlay, pink over white, the pink partly removed to form three oval white panels, engraved with a running rabbit, a running dog, and two birds in flight; the top with a circular window, revealing an upright bouquet of flowers and foliage, a white flower at the top; the bottom of the weight star-cut.

D. 8.2 cm (3⁷/₃₂ in.)
Mr. and Mrs. Paul Jokelson, New York, New York
Fluorescence: cloudy, coral-pink
Color illustration, page 89

**213. France, Saint-Louis (attrib.), ca. 1845-55**
Encased double overlay, pink over white, with six interior circular windows on the sides and one on the top; revealing an upright bouquet of flowers and foliage, a bright yellow and blue flower at the top; the bottom of the weight star-cut.

D. 7.3 cm (2²⁷/₃₂ in.)
Private collection
Fluorescence: cloudy, coral-pink
Color illustration, page 89

**214. France, Saint-Louis (attrib.), ca. 1845-55**
Encased double overlay, white over translucent salmon, with six interior circular windows on the sides and one on the top; revealing an upright bouquet of flowers and foliage, a white flower at the top; the bottom of the weight star-cut.

D. 6.9 cm (2¾ in.)
The Corning Museum of Glass (No. 55.3.114; gift of the Hon. Amory Houghton, Sr.)
Fluorescence: cloudy, pale coral-pink
Color illustration, page 89

**215. France, Saint-Louis (attrib.), ca. 1845-55**
Encased triple overlay, dark blue over white over transparent salmon, with interior circular windows on the top and sides; revealing a small upright bouquet of flowers and foliage, a small red flower at the top; the bottom of the weight star-cut.

D. 8.1 cm (3⅛ in.)
The Corning Museum of Glass (No. 55.3.90; gift of the Hon. Amory Houghton, Sr.)
Fluorescence: cloudy, pale coral-pink
Color illustration, page 89

*The only recorded encased triple overlay paperweight.*

**216. France, Saint-Louis (attrib.), ca. 1845-55**
Encased double overlay, dark blue over white, the blue partially removed to form alternating white and blue vertical panels, with small cut circular windows and stars on the panels; a large circular window on the top; revealing an upright bouquet of flowers and foliage, a large orange flower at the top; the bottom of the weight star-cut.

D. 7.6 cm (3 in.)
The John Nelson Bergstrom Art Center and Museum, Neenah, Wisconsin (No. 219)
Fluorescence: cloudy, coral-pink
Color illustration, page 90

COMPAGNIE DES CRISTALLERIES DE SAINT-LOUIS

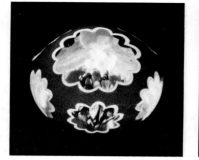

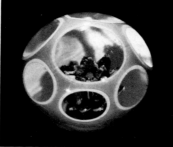

**217. France, Saint-Louis (attrib.), ca. 1845-55**
Encased double overlay, blue over white, with five interior scalloped windows on the sides and one on the top, revealing an upright bouquet of flowers and foliage, a red flower at the top.

D. 8.2 cm (3⁷/₃₂ in.)
Private collection
Fluorescence: cloudy, coral-pink
Color illustration, page 90

**218. France, Saint-Louis (attrib.), ca. 1845-55**
Encased double overlay, turquoise blue over white, with six interior circular windows on the sides and one on the top, revealing an upright bouquet of flowers and foliage, a large orange-red flower at the top.

D. 7.5 (2¹⁵/₁₆ in.)
The Corning Museum of Glass (No. 54.3.175; bequest of Ellen D. Sharpe)
Fluorescence: cloudy, coral-pink
Color illustration, page 90

**219. France, Saint-Louis (attrib.), ca. 1845-55**
Encased double overlay, bright yellow-green over white, with six interior circular windows on the sides and one on the top, revealing an upright bouquet of flowers and foliage, a blue flower at the top; the bottom of the weight star-cut.

D. 8.0 cm (3⁵/₃₂ in.)
The Corning Museum of Glass (No. 57.3.186; gift of the Hon. Amory Houghton, Sr.)
Fluorescence: cloudy, pale coral-pink
Color illustration, page 90

**220. France, Saint-Louis (attrib.), ca. 1845-55**
Encased double overlay, aventurine-flecked yellow-green over white, with six interior circular windows on the sides and one on the top, revealing an upright bouquet of flowers and foliage, a large ribbed pink flower at the top; the bottom of the weight star-cut.

D. 7.0 cm (2¾ in.)
The Corning Museum of Glass (No. 69.3.79; gift of the Hon. Amory Houghton, Sr.)
Fluorescence: cloudy, coral-pink
Color illustration, page 90

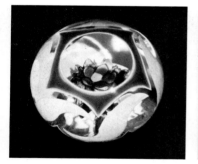

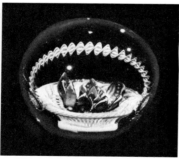

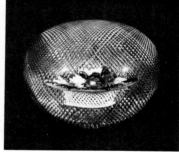

**221. France, Saint-Louis (attrib.), ca. 1845-55**
Encased double overlay, dark green over white, with a cut circular window in a narrow pentagonal frame; a running band of white S-scrolls on the sides, and a green pentagonal frame with circular window at the base; enclosing an upright bouquet of flowers and green foliage, a red flower at the center; the bottom of the weight star-cut.

D. 7.3 cm (2⅞ in.)
Private collection
Fluorescence: cloudy, coral-pink
Color illustration, page 90

**222. France, probably, Saint-Louis, ca. 1845-55**
Double-spiral white lattice basket with amber and white twisted rim and blue, amber, and white twisted handle with blue and white canes at the terminals; containing an upright bouquet of flowers and foliage.

D. 8.0 cm (3⅛ in.)
The John Nelson Bergstrom Art Center and Museum, Neenah, Wisconsin (No. 1013; gift of Mrs. Florence Gosselin Marsh in memory of her husband, Raymond Clark Marsh)
Fluorescence: cloudy, pink
Color illustration, page 91

*The fluorescence is not as boldly "coral" as in other Saint-Louis weights.*

**223. France, Saint-Louis (attrib.), ca. 1845-55**
Double-spiral white lattice "basket" with red and white twisted handle with millefiori terminals, containing an upright bouquet of flowers and foliage.

D. 7.8 cm (3¹/₁₆ in.)
The Corning Museum of Glass (No. 63.3.36; gift of the Hon. Amory Houghton, Sr.)
Fluorescence: cloudy, coral-pink
Color illustration, page 91

**224. France, probably, Saint-Louis, ca. 1845-55**
A bisected large weight, the flat side diamond-faceted; enclosing a double-spiral white lattice basket with yellow and white spiral twist rim; containing an upright bouquet of flowers and foliage.

H. 10.5 cm (4⅛ in.); W. 14.0 cm (5½ in.); Depth 6.9 cm (2¾ in.)
The John Nelson Bergstrom Art Center and Museum, Neenah, Wisconsin (No.1012; gift of Mrs. Florence Gosselin Marsh in memory of her husband, Raymond Clark Marsh)
Fluorescence: cloudy, pink
Color illustration, page 91

*The fluorescence is not so "coral" as in other Saint-Louis weights.*

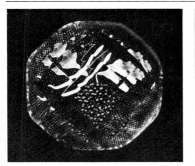

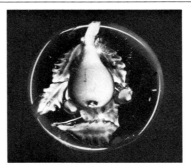

**225. France, Saint-Louis (attrib.), ca. 1845-55**

A bunch of purple grapes hanging from an amber branch, with green leaves; square faceting on the top and circular facets on the sides of the weight; the bottom diamond-faceted.

D. 7.9 cm (3³/₃₂ in.)
Private collection, courtesy of Alan Tillman (Antiques) Ltd., London
Fluorescence: cloudy, coral-pink
Color illustration, page 97

**226. France, Saint-Louis (attrib.), ca. 1845-55**

Two red cherries on yellow stems and an amber branch, with green leaves; cut hexagonal facets on the top and sides of the weight; the bottom of the weight with finely-cut small diamonds.

D. 9.3 cm (3¹¹/₁₆ in.)
Private collection, courtesy of Spink & Son, Ltd., London
Fluorescence: cloudy, coral-pink
Color illustration, page 97

**227. France, Saint-Louis (attrib.), ca. 1845-55**

Realistic pear and three cherries, with ribbed green foliage.

D. 4.5 cm (1¹³/₁₆ in.)
Mr. and Mrs. Franklin Schuell, South Bend, Indiana
Fluorescence: cloudy, coral-pink
Color illustration, page 98

**228. France, Saint-Louis (attrib.), ca. 1845-55**

Three pears, three cherries, and green leaves symmetrically disposed on a double spiral white lattice ground; six cut circular facets on the sides of the weight and one on the top.

D. 8.1 cm (3³/₁₆ in.)
The John Nelson Bergstrom Art Center and Museum, Neenah, Wisconsin (No. 1069; gift of Mrs. Florence Gosselin Marsh in memory of her husband, Raymond Clark Marsh)
Fluorescence: cloudy, coral-pink
Color illustration, page 98

**229. France, Saint-Louis (attrib.), ca. 1845-55**

White swan on undulating, striped, pale blue water, with the edge of a green "bank"(?) at one end; a pink and blue spiral twist set into the side of the weight; the bottom diamond-faceted.

D. 8.1 cm (3³/₁₆ in.)
Private collection
Fluorescence: cloudy, coral-pink
Color illustration, page 102

**230. France, Saint-Louis (attrib.), ca. 1845-55**

Brilliantly colored parrot with blue and yellow speckled body, and red, yellow, and white wings; perched on a holly branch with two green leaves and red berries; a red and white spiral twist set into the side of the weight; the bottom diamond-faceted.

D. 7.9 cm (3³/₃₂ in.)
Private collection
Fluorescence: cloudy, coral-pink
Color illustration, page 102

**231. France, Saint-Louis (attrib.), ca. 1845-55**

Butterfly with brilliant green wings decorated with millefiori canes and ribbons, and a green- and orange-striped frog; a red and white spiral twist set into the side of the weight; the bottom diamond-faceted.

D. 8.0 cm (3¹/₈ in.)
Private collection, courtesy of Alan Tillman (Antiques) Ltd., London
Fluorescence: cloudy, coral-pink
Color illustration, page 102

**232. France, Saint-Louis (attrib.), ca. 1845-55**

Blown weight; blushed, yellow fruit (possibly an apple), the blossom end a blue and white lattice cane; on a colorless square "pillow."

H. 9.3 cm (3¹¹/₁₆ in.); W. 9.8 cm (3⁷/₈ in.)
Old Sturbridge Village, Sturbridge, Massachusetts (No. 8.34)
Fluorescence: cloudy, coral-pink
Color illustration, page 99

*A similar blown fruit was given to the Conservatoire des Arts et Métiers, Paris, in January 1851. It was described as a "Presse-papiers, pomme sur socle."*

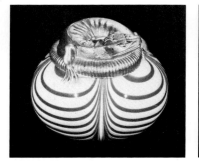

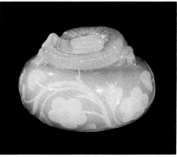

### 233. France, Saint-Louis (attrib.), ca. 1845-55

Blown, hollow weight, with a molded, gilded, coiled lizard on a bulbous base, decorated with blue swags on a white background.

D. 8.5 cm (3¹¹/₃₂ in.)
Illinois State Museum, Springfield (No.702426; gift of Morton D. Barker)
Fluorescence: too thin to be apparent
Color illustration, page 106

*The lizard has been regilded; apparently unique in the use of "marbrie." See also nos. 234 and 235.*

### 234. France, Saint-Louis (attrib.), ca. 1845-55

Blown and molded overlay weight (pink over opalescent white ["opaline"]) of a molded, coiled lizard atop a bulbous base; the sides of the base decorated with a cut undulating vine with leaves and flowers; a hole drilled in the bottom.

D. 8.8 cm (3¹⁵/₃₂ in.)
The John Nelson Bergstrom Art Center and Museum, Neenah, Wisconsin (No. 209)
Fluorescence of the "opaline": gray-green
Color illustration, page 106

*Blown into a three-part, hinged mold; the top part of the lizard was formed by the base-plate of the mold. See also nos. 233 and 235.*

### 235. France, Saint-Louis (attrib.), ca. 1845-55

Blown, double overlay weight, green over white on colorless; of a molded, gilded, coiled lizard on a bulbous base, the sides decorated with gilded scrolls and a cut, undulating vine with leaves and flowers.

D. 8.9 cm (3½ in.)
The Art Institute of Chicago (gift of Arthur Rubloff, No. 468)
Fluorescence of colorless glass: cloudy, coral-pink
Color illustration, page 106

*A similar weight was given by the Compagnie des Cristalleries de Saint-Louis to the Conservatoire des*

*Arts et Métiers, Paris, in January 1851. It was described as a "Presse-papiers lézard, triplé vert, taillé, huit pointils, décoré." See also nos. 233 and 234.*

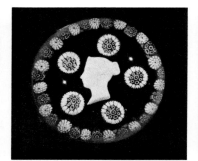

### 236. France, Saint-Louis (attrib.), ca. 1845-55

Sulphide profile portrait of the young Queen Victoria, inscribed "Victoria" in blue script; five white, pink, and blue canes around the portrait, encircled with a ring of alternating yellow and blue canes; the bottom of the weight amber-stained.

D. 6.5 cm (2⁹/₁₆ in.)
The John Nelson Bergstrom Art Center and Museum, Neenah, Wisconsin (No. 361)
Fluorescence: cloudy, coral-pink
Color illustration, page 115

### 237. France, Saint-Louis (attrib.), ca. 1845-55

Sulphide portrait of Louis Bonaparte, inscribed on the plinth, encircled by a ring of alternating blue and pink canes; the sides of the weight cut with flat panels, the top with a ten-sided facet; the bottom with cross-hatched diamond cutting, amber-stained.

D. 8.4 cm (3⁹/₃₂ in.)
Illinois State Museum, Springfield (No. 702476; gift of Morton D. Barker)
Fluorescence: cloudy, coral-pink
Color illustration, page 118

### 238. France, Saint-Louis, 1867

Weight with circular facets on the sides and top; the bottom of the weight amber-stained and engraved with the foliated initials "ED," enclosing a medal of the Legion of Honor; encircled by a wreath of laurel.

D. 11.6 cm (4⁹/₁₆ in.)
Mr. and Mrs. Gérard Ingold, Paris
Fluorescence: cloudy, gray-blue
Color illustration, page 119

*Made in 1867 for Mr. Eugène Didierjean, General Manager of the Saint-Louis manufactory; it is owned by his great grandson, one of the Directors of Saint-Louis. Other, similar weights are in the museum of the Great Chancellor of the Legion of Honor in Paris. An im-*

*portant weight for its obvious quality and in that it documents other weights of this type. There are also few weights dated later than the 1845-55 period which can be documented as to manufacturer. Note that the fluorescence is entirely different from the earlier (1845-55) period weights from Saint-Louis.*

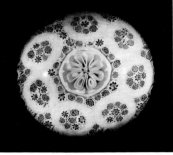

**George Bacchus & Sons, Union Glass Works, Birmingham, England Founded 1818; ownership changed 1860**

**Documented paperweight products: nothing signed known.**

**239. England, George Bacchus and Sons (attrib.), Birmingham, ca. 1845-55**
Garland of panels of red and white canes, encircled by rings of translucent white "sodden snow," bordered by red and white canes; a large ruffled white cane at the center; the perimeter edged with blue-lined ribbed white canes, drawn together at the center of the base.

D. 8.5 cm (3⁵/₁₆ in.)
The New-York Historical Society (No. 1965.437.BS; bequest of Mrs. Jennie H. Sinclair)
Fluorescence: cloudy, lime-green
Color illustration, page 36

**240. England, George Bacchus and Sons (attrib.), Birmingham, ca. 1845-55**
Carpet of pale blue and white, ruffled and lacy canes, arranged in concentric bands, around a large ruffled white cane inside a hemispherical cup at the center.

D. 8.8 cm (3⁷/₁₆ in.)
Private collection
Fluorescence: bright, lime-green
Color illustration, page 36

*The central cane seems to have an internal wire.*

**241. England, George Bacchus and Sons (attrib.), Birmingham, ca. 1845-55**
Mushroom with concentric rings of blue, green, white and pink ruffled canes around a central ruffled red and white cane; encircled with a blue and white spiral *torsade* at the base.

D. 8.7 cm (3⁷/₁₆ in.)
The John Nelson Bergstrom Art Center and Museum, Neenah, Wisconsin (No. 203)
Fluorescence: bright, yellow-green
Color illustration, page 45

*The* torsade *twists to the right on Bacchus weights.*

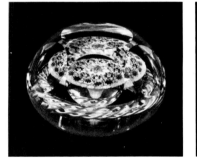

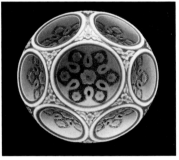

**242. England, George Bacchus and Sons (attrib.), Birmingham, ca. 1845-55**
Mushroom with concentric rings of red-, green-, and blue-lined white crimped canes, with an outer ring of white canes; encircled by a red and white spiral *torsade* at the base; six large cut circular facets on the sides of the weight and one on the top; the bottom star-cut.

D. 9.1 cm (3¹⁹/₃₂ in.)
The Art Institute of Chicago (gift of Arthur Rubloff, No. 333)
Fluorescence: bright, yellow-green
Color illustration, page 45

**243. England, George Bacchus and Sons (attrib.), Birmingham, ca. 1845-55**
Ribbed pink and white basket with five concentric rings of red, white, and blue crimped canes in the top; twisted red, white, and blue loop handles at either side.

D. 9.1 cm (3⁹/₁₆ in.)
The Art Institute of Chicago (gift of Arthur Rubloff, No. 86)
Fluorescence: Cloudy, gray-tan; some of the stripes on the basket fluoresce a brilliant yellow-green
Color illustration, page 42

**244. England, probably, Stourbridge, ca. 1880-90**
Triple overlay weight, white over red over white, with six cut circular windows on the sides and one on the top, the spaces between decorated with cameo-carved flowers; the bottom of the weight carved with a six-petaled flower, with small cameo flowers in each petal.

D. 7.2 cm (2³⁷/₃₂ in.)
The Corning Museum of Glass (No. 56.3.196; gift of the Hon. Amory Houghton, Sr.)
Fluorescence: cloudy gray
Color illustration, page 119

**245. England (?), Birmingham-Stourbridge area, possibly George Bacchus and Sons, ca. 1845-55**
White overlay, with cut circular oval and diamond-shaped windows on the sides, and one on the top, revealing an encased overlay plaque of five layers: white/green/white/red/white; with sprays of berries and leaves cut through to expose various layers.

D. 8.8 cm (3⁷/₁₆ in.)
The New-York Historical Society (No. 1965.319.E; bequest of Mrs. Jennie H. Sinclair)
Fluorescence: bright yellow
Color illustration, page 113

*There are no known parallels for this extraordinary weight.*

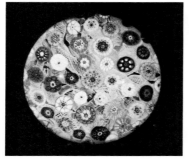

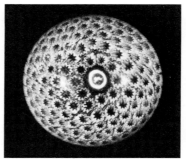

**New England Glass Company, East Cambridge, Massachusetts**
**Founded 1818; closed in 1888 and moved to Toledo, Ohio**

**Documented paperweight products: nothing signed known; dated 1852 and 1854 (millefiori weights).**

**246. United States, New England Glass Company (attrib.), Cambridge, Massachusetts, ca. 1852-80**
Spaced millefiori canes on a filigree ground.

D. 9.1 cm (3⁹/₁₆ in.)
The Art Institute of Chicago (gift of Arthur Rubloff, No. 594)
Fluorescence: cloudy, gray-tan
Color illustration, page 29

*The fluorescence is similar to that of the Bacchus basket, no. 243.*

**247. United States, New England Glass Company (attrib.), Cambridge, Massachusetts, ca. 1852-80**
Domed carpet of red and white crimped canes, with a black and white rabbit silhouette cane at the center.

D. 6.8 cm (2¹¹/₁₆ in.)
Old Sturbridge Village, Sturbridge, Massachusetts (No. 8.49)
Fluorescence: cloudy, yellow-green
Color illustration, page 34

**248. United States, New England Glass Company (attrib.), Cambridge, Massachusetts, ca. 1852-80**
Opaque white drum, the domed, translucent top with inset pink, white, turquoise, and green canes; opaque white overlay with cut circular, quatrefoil, and trefoil facets on the sides and top, and two bands of slanted ovals at the base.

D. 8.5 cm (3⁵/₁₆ in.)
The John Nelson Bergstrom Art Center and Museum, Neenah, Wisconsin (No. 168)
Fluorescence: cloudy, pale lime-green
Color illustration, page 45

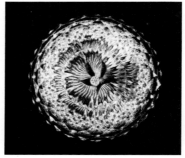

**249. United States, New England Glass Company (attrib.), Cambridge, Massachusetts, ca. 1852-80**
Flat bouquet of three cane flowers and green leaves set into the domed top of a white mushroom, the rim set with pink, white, and blue canes; white and mauve double overlay, with a cut circular window on the top; oval, circular, and quatrefoil windows on the sides; and vertical fluting at the base.

D. 8.1 cm (3³/₁₆ in.)
The New-York Historical Society (No. 1965.298.NE; bequest of Mrs. Jennie H. Sinclair)
Fluorescence: cloudy, lime-green
Color illustration, page 60

**250. United States, possibly New England Glass Company, Cambridge, Massachusetts, ca. 1852-80**
Flat bouquet of three cane flowers and green leaves, above an open cup of pink, blue, white, and yellow canes, drawn together at the base; a circular cut facet at the top of the weight, and diamond-faceted sides.

D. 8.0 cm (3¹/₈ in.)
The John Nelson Bergstrom Art Center and Museum, Neenah, Wisconsin (No. 195)
Fluorescence: bright yellow-green
Color illustration, page 60

**251. United States, New England Glass Company (attrib.), Cambridge, Massachusetts, ca. 1852-80**
Spray of three cane flowers and green leaves, on a double spiral white lattice ground, ringed with circles of millefiori canes; white and black (dark blue) double overlay, elaborately cut with a circular window on the top and fluted and hexagonally-cut leaves about the sides.

D. 7.0 cm (2³/₄ in.)
Arthur Rubloff collection, No. 990
Fluorescence: not tested
Color illustration, page 60

*The extraordinarily elaborate cutting on this weight is paralleled in no. 256.*

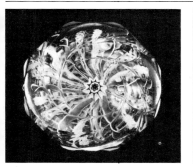

**252. United States, probably New England Glass Company or Boston and Sandwich Glass Company, Massachusetts, ca. 1852**
Hollow "crown" of colored and white filigree twists; with a black and white star cane at the center, inscribed "1825"; with a cut circular facet on the top and spiral cut flutes, and circular and quatrefoil facets on the sides of the weight.

D. 6.5 cm (2¹⁷/₃₂ in.)
The John Nelson Bergstrom Art Center and Museum, Neenah, Wisconsin (No. 310)
Fluorescence: cloudy, pale lime-green
Color illustration, page 56

**253. United States, New England Glass Company (attrib.), Cambridge, Massachusetts, ca. 1852-80**
White, five-petaled, circular flower (buttercup) with five-pointed yellow and white star-shaped center cane, green stem and leaves, and a white and green bud; encircled by a ring of alternating pink and dark purple canes; the bottom of the weight star-cut.

D. 7.4 cm (2²⁹/₃₂ in.)
Private collection
Fluorescence: cloudy, pale lime-green; the yellow center fluoresces a brilliant yellow-green
Color illustration, page 69

**254. United States, New England Glass Company (attrib.), Cambridge, Massachusetts, ca. 1852-80**
Cross formed of overlapping green leaves, with a white flower at the center; on a double spiral white lattice ground; cut triangular and square facets on the sides of the weight and one circular facet on the top.

D. 8.3 cm (3¹/₄ in.)
The John Nelson Bergstrom Art Center and Museum, Neenah, Wisconsin (No. 128)
Fluorescence: bright yellow-green
Color illustration, page 93

**255. United States, New England Glass Company (attrib.), Cambridge, Massachusetts, ca. 1852-80**
Sheaf of flowers, foliage, and fruit; on a double spiral white lattice ground.

D. 10.1 cm (4 in.)
The Hon. and Mrs. Amory Houghton, Sr., Corning, New York
Fluorescence: cloudy, greenish-yellow
Color illustration, page 93

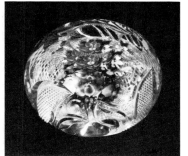

**256. United States, New England Glass Company (attrib.), Cambridge, Massachusetts, ca. 1852-80**
Sheaf of flowers, fruit, and foliage, in a striped lavender "posy" holder, on a double spiral white lattice ground; the weight elaborately cut, with circles on the top and fluted and hexagonally-cut leaves about the sides.

D. 10.4 cm (4³/₃₂ in.)
Mr. and Mrs. Bernard Moos, Jr.
Fluorescence: cloudy, lime-green
Color illustration, page 93

*See also no. 251.*

**257. United States, New England Glass Company (attrib.), Cambridge, Massachusetts, ca. 1852-80**
Flat "posy" with three cane blossoms, stems, and leaves, encircled by five pink and yellow pears; a cut circular facet on the top of the weight.

D. 7.2 cm (2¹³/₁₆ in.)
The Art Institute of Chicago (gift of Arthur Rubloff, No. 760)
Fluorescence: gray
Color illustration, page 98

**258. United States, probably New England Glass Company, Cambridge, Massachusetts, ca. 1860-80**
Blown, bulbous, spotted red and pink apple, with curved green stem.

D. 7.5 cm (2¹⁵/₁₆ in.)
Old Sturbridge Village, Sturbridge, Massachusetts (No. 8.36.J)
Fluorescence: not applicable (no colorless glass)
Color illustration, page 99

**259. United States, New England Glass Company (attrib.), Cambridge, Massachusetts, ca. 1860-80**
Blown, spherical, striped russet and yellow apple, fused to a colorless circular disk foot.

D. 7.8 cm (3¹/₁₆ in.)
Old Sturbridge Village, Sturbridge, Massachusetts (No. 8.36.B)
Fluorescence (pad): gray
Color illustration, page 99

**Boston & Sandwich Glass Company, Sandwich, Massachusetts**
**Founded 1825; closed 1888**
**Documented paperweight products: nothing signed by the factory known; "dated" 1825 and 1852.**

**260. United States, Boston & Sandwich Glass Company (attrib.), Sandwich, Massachusetts, ca. 1852-80**
Wheatflower with overlapping, blue-speckled, white petals; with a white and red cane cluster at the center; green stem and leaves.

D. 7.3 cm (2⅞ in.)
Private collection
Fluorescence: bright yellow-green
Color illustration, page 65

*Flowers such as this are frequently attributed to Nicholas Lutz, but there were probably other lampworkers equally skilled.*

**261. United States, possibly Boston & Sandwich Glass Company, Sandwich, Massachusetts, ca. 1852-80**
Red-and-white and red-and-black ribbed, multi-petaled flower with green aventurine spots on the petals; cane cluster at the center; ribbed green leaves.

D. 5.5 cm (2⁵/₃₂ in.)
Private collection
Fluorescence: pale lime-green
Color illustration, page 66

**262. United States, Boston & Sandwich Glass Company (attrib.), Sandwich, Massachusetts, ca. 1852-80**
A flower with pointed, overlapping blue and pink petals; pink and white cane center; green stem and leaves.

D. 7.1 cm (2²⁵/₃₂ in.)
Dr. and Mrs. Daniel S. Turner, New York
Fluorescence: cloudy, bright yellow-green
Color illustration, page 66

**263. United States, Boston & Sandwich Glass Company (attrib.), Sandwich, Massachusetts, ca. 1852-80**
Three red- and yellow-striped fruits and four veined green leaves.

D. 5.1 cm (2 in.)
Mr. and Mrs. Franklin Schuell, South Bend, Indiana
Fluorescence: bright yellow-green
Color illustration, page 97

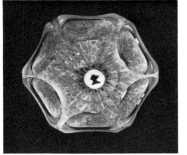

**Gillinder & Sons, Philadelphia, Pennsylvania**
**Founded 1861; closed 1930**

**Documented paperweight products: signed pressed weights; no signed millefiori examples known.**

**264. United States, Gillinder & Sons, Philadelphia, ca. 1861-70**
Carpet ground of blue lacy canes, with a ring of ribbed red canes surrounding a profile female portrait (said to be Queen Victoria) at the center; a ring of ribbed white canes at the base; six deep oval cut facets on the sides and a circular cut facet on the top.
D. 7.8 cm (3¹/₁₆ in.)
Emma Gillinder Masland
Fluorescence: bright yellow-green
Color illustration, page 34

*Owned by a descendant of the maker, who also has a length of the silhouette cane used in the center of this weight. The profile cane may have been brought to America from the Birmingham, England, area by William T. Gillinder.*

**265. United States, Gillinder & Sons, Philadelphia (attrib.), ca. 1861-70**
Close concentric millefiori weight with crimped polychrome canes; the weight with six deep oval cut facets on the sides and a circular facet on top.
D. 7.8 cm (3¹/₁₆ in.)
Private collection
Fluorescence: Cloudy, pale lime-green; several canes fluoresce a brilliant yellow-green
Color illustration, page 34

**Mount Washington Glass Company, South Boston and (later) New Bedford, Massachusetts**
**Founded 1837; closed 1957 (after numerous changes in ownership and interruptions)**

**Documented paperweight products: nothing signed known.**

**266. United States, Mount Washington Glass Company (attrib.), New Bedford, Massachusetts, ca. 1870-90**
Large poinsettia with veined red bracts, and an orange and blue flower within; green stem and veined green leaves.
D. 8.5 cm (3¹¹/₃₂ in.)
The John Nelson Bergstrom Art Center and Museum, Neenah, Wisconsin (No. 516)
Fluorescence: bright lime-green
Color illustration, page 66

**267. United States, Mount Washington Glass Company (attrib.), New Bedford, Massachusetts, ca. 1870-90**
Massive rose with pink petals, two buds and green leaves.
D. 10.9 cm (4⁵/₁₆ in.)
The New-York Historical Society (No. 1965.331.MW; bequest of Mrs. Jennie H. Sinclair)
Fluorescence: cloudy, pale gray-blue
Color illustration, page 82

**268. United States, Mount Washington Glass Company (attrib.), New Bedford, Massachusetts, ca. 1870-90**
Large, three dimensional pink and yellow rose, two buds and veined green leaves.
D. 10.8 cm (4¹/₄ in.)
Dr. and Mrs. Daniel S. Turner, New York
Fluorescence: bright yellow-green
Color illustration, page 83

**269. United States, Mount Washington Glass Company (attrib.), New Bedford, Massachusetts, ca. 1870-90**
Large rose with mottled pink, orange, and white serrated petals, with two buds; the green stem grasped by a pink hand wearing a gold ring; three multi-colored butterflies with cane wings hover above the flower; four small cut circular facets on the sides of the weight.

D. 11.0 cm (4⅝ in.)
Old Sturbridge Village, Sturbridge, Massachusetts (No. 8.26)
Fluorescence: cloudy, bright blue
Color illustration, page 83

**270. United States, possibly Mount Washington Glass Company, New Bedford, Massachusetts, ca. 1870-90**
Rectangular plaque with cut, canted corners and sides, enclosing a large formal bouquet of thirteen red, pink, yellow, lavender, and dark and light blue flowers and leaves; the stems tied together with a red ribbon.

L. 13.6 cm (5⅜ in.); W. 9.1 cm (3⁹/₁₆ in.) Depth 3.6 cm (1⁷/₁₆ in.)
Private collection
Fluorescence: cloudy, tan; the yellow flowers and the centers of all of the flowers fluoresce a brilliant yellow-green
Color illustration, page 85

**271. United States, probably Massachusetts, possibly Mount Washington Glass Company, New Bedford, Massachusetts, ca. 1870-90**
A dark red strawberry with pink seeds and green leaves at the center, encircled by four similar strawberries alternating with four white flowers.

D. 10.0 cm (3¹⁵/₁₆ in.)
Private collection
Fluorescence: cloudy, bright lime-green
Color illustration, page 96

**272. United States, possibly Mount Washington Glass Company, New Bedford, Massachusetts, late nineteenth century**
Seal of flat shield shape, containing four ovoid wild strawberries on green stems; with blue and yellow flowers, two on each face; blue and white ribbon; panel-cut stem and polished flat pad.

H. 10.8 cm (4¼ in.); W. 4.5 cm (1¾ in.)
Mr. and Mrs. Franklin Schuell, South Bend, Indiana
Fluorescence: cloudy, yellow-green; the yellow flower fluoresces a brilliant yellow-green
Color illustration, page 96

**273. United States, possibly Mount Washington Glass Company, New Bedford, Massachusetts, ca. 1870-90**
Seven red strawberries on green stems, a white flower at the center and two buds above; veined green leaves.

D. 11.5 cm (4½ in.)
Private collection
Fluorescence: cloudy, lime-green
Color illustration, page 96

*Said to have belonged to the president of the Union Glass Company, Somerville, Massachusetts, but the leaves and stems are similar to those in weights attributed to the Mount Washington Glass Company.*

**Whitall Tatum Company, Millville, New Jersey**
Founded ca. 1806; operating today under different ownership
Documented paperweight products: nothing signed.

**274. United States, Whitall Tatum Company (attrib.), Millville, New Jersey, early twentieth century**
Yellow-centered water lily with pink, tubular stamens, white petals and green sepals; disk foot.

D. 8.5 cm (3⁵/₁₆ in.)
The John Nelson Bergstrom Art Center and Museum, Neenah, Wisconsin (No. 237)
Fluorescence: brilliant yellow
Color illustration, page 79

**275. United States, Whitall Tatum Company (attrib.), Millville, New Jersey, probably made by Ralph Barber, early twentieth century**
A pink rose and green leaves, tilted in a colorless sphere; on a baluster stem and disk foot.

D. 8.8 cm (3⁷/₁₆ in.); H. 15.0 cm (5¹⁵/₁₆ in.)
The John Nelson Bergstrom Art Center and Museum, Neenah, Wisconsin (No. 328)
Fluorescence: brilliant yellow
Color illustration, page 82

**276. United States (?), factory unknown, late nineteenth century**
Scattered flowers, including morning glories; domed, cut top and diamond-cut sides.

D. 9.8 cm (3⁷/₈ in.)
The John Nelson Bergstrom Art Center and Museum, Neenah, Wisconsin (No. 542)
Fluorescence: cloudy, lime-green
Color illustration, page 85

**277. Belgium, Val Saint-Lambert (attrib.), Seraing, near Liège, ca. 1850-1900**
A flower with seven petals, the upper surfaces with pink, blue, green, white, and red looped bands, the underside white; green stem and leaves; encircled by a spiral ribbon *torsade* in colors matching the petals; the bottom of the weight star-cut.

D. 7.8 cm (3¹/₁₆ in.)
The New-York Historical Society (No. 1965.430.VL; bequest of Mrs. Jennie H. Sinclair)
Fluorescence: cloudy, pale pink
Color illustration, page 63

**278. France, factory unknown, late nineteenth century**
Yellow-green coiled salamander with spotted skin; on a green and tan sandy ground.

D. 11.5 cm (4¹/₂ in.)
The Corning Museum of Glass (No. 55.3.79; gift of the Hon. Amory Houghton, Sr.)
Fluorescence: cloudy, gray-green
Color illustration, page 107

**279. France, factory unknown, late nineteenth century**
Coiled yellow-green salamander with spotted skin; on a green, tan, and white sandy ground; two plants at the side, one with a pink, the other with a yellow flower.

D. 10.7 cm (4¹⁵/₃₂ in.)
Private collection
Fluorescence: cloudy, bluish-green
Color illustration, page 108

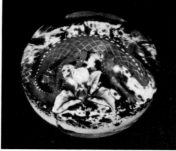

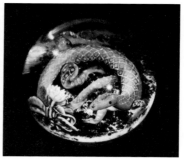

### 280. France, factory unknown, late nineteenth century

Coiled yellow-green salamander with spotted skin; on a green, tan, and white sandy ground; a plant at one side with a white and yellow flower, and a black- and yellow-striped bumblebee whose wings are formed of oval pads of tiny bubbles.

D. 10.7 cm (4⁷⁄₃₂ in.)
The John Nelson Bergstrom Art Center and Museum, Neenah, Wisconsin (No. 230)
Fluorescence: cloudy, gray-green
Color illustration, page 108

### 281. France, factory unknown, late nineteenth century

Coiled green salamander with yellow scales on the sides and legs and spots on the spine; on a green, tan, and white sandy ground; a plant at the side, with yellow buttercup flower and green leaves.

D. 10.6 cm (4³⁄₁₆ in.)
Dr. and Mrs. Junius T. Langston, Plainfield, New Jersey
Fluorescence: not recorded
Color illustration, page 109

### 282. France, factory unknown, late nineteenth century

Coiled orange-red salamander with yellow scales and green spots, on a green, tan, and white sandy ground; a plant with a yellow flower and green foliage at the side.

D. 10.5 cm (4⅛ in.)
Illinois State Museum, Springfield (No. 702399; gift of Morton D. Barker)
Fluorescence: cloudy, bluish-green
Color illustration, page 110

### 283. France, factory unknown, late nineteenth century

Coiled dark orange-red salamander with green scales and spots, on a green, tan, and white sandy ground; a plant at the side with a small red and white flower and yellow-edged green foliage.

D. 10.7 cm (4³⁄₁₆ in.)
The Art Institute of Chicago (gift of Arthur Rubloff, No. 331)
Fluorescence: cloudy, gray-green
Color illustration, page 110

*The plant may be a representation of an aloe.*

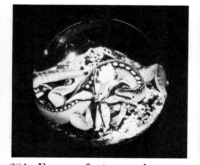

### 284. France, factory unknown, late nineteenth century

Coiled orange-red salamander with a yellow-spotted dark stripe down the back, and with yellow scales; on a green, tan, and white sandy ground; a plant with white flower and green leaves at the center.

D. 10.7 cm (4¼ in.)
Private collection
Fluorescence: cloudy, bluish-green
Color illustration, page 109

### 285. France, factory unknown, late nineteenth century

Coiled, silver-flecked black salamander with tan spots and diamond scales on the back and legs; on a green, tan, and white sandy ground; two plants with yellow buttercup flowers and green foliage at the sides.

D. 10.4 cm (4¹⁄₁₆ in.)
Mr. and Mrs. Paul Jokelson, New York, New York
Fluorescence: ashy, bluish-green
Color illustration, page 111

*One of the plants seems to be an aloe.*

### 286. France, factory unknown, late nineteenth century

Silver-flecked, coiled black salamander on a green and white sandy ground; a plant with yellow buttercup flower and green foliage at the side.

D. 11.3 cm (4⅜ in.)
The Corning Museum of Glass (No. 56.3.199; gift of the Hon. Amory Houghton, Sr.)
Fluorescence: cloudy, bluish-green
Color illustration, page 111

### 287. France, factory unknown, late nineteenth century

Four mauve-colored silkworms on a partially-eaten green mulberry leaf; above radiating white filigree rods and a brilliant blue ground.

D. 9.2 cm (3¹⁹⁄₃₂ in.)
Mr. and Mrs. Paul Jokelson, New York, New York
Fluorescence: ashy, bluish-green
Color illustration, page 105

*The fluorescence of this weight is similar to that of some of the salamander weights (nos. 278-286). An apparently unique representation, and an impressive foray into naturalism.*

**288. France, factory unknown, late nineteenth century**
Two white daisies with green and yellow centers; with one bud, green stems and notched and veined leaves; on a double spiral white lattice ground.

D. 8.4 cm (3⁹/₃₂ in.)
The John Nelson Bergstrom Art Center and Museum, Neenah, Wisconsin (No. 136)
Fluorescence: cloudy, gray-green
Color illustration, page 79

*The fluorescence is similar to that of some of the salamander weights (nos. 278-286).*

**289. France, factory unknown, ca. 1870-80**
Three-dimensional, multi-petaled pink rose with green sepals, pink and green bud, green leaves and stem; brilliant blue ground.

D. 7.9 cm (3⅛ in.)
Private collection
Fluorescence: cloudy, gray-green
Color illustration, page 80

*The fluorescence of this weight is similar to that of some of the salamander weights (nos. 278-286). It is dissimilar to Clichy weights.*

**290. France, factory unknown, late nineteenth century**
A three-dimensional pink and yellow bird perched on a green branch with foliage, beside a green nest which holds three brilliant blue eggs.

D. 9.0 cm (3¹⁷/₃₂ in.)
Mr. and Mrs. Paul Jokelson, New York, New York
Fluorescence: cloudy, bluish-gray
Color illustration, page 103

*The fluorescence is different from that found in the salamander weights.*

**291. France, factory unknown, ca. 1870-80**
Large white rose and two buds; green stem and leaves; pink ground.

D. 6.7 cm (2⅝ in.)
The New-York Historical Society (No. 1965.353.U; bequest of Mrs. Jennie H. Sinclair)
Fluorescence: brilliant yellow-green

Color illustration, page 81

*This, and the next five weights, are usually attributed to the Monot, père et fils et Stumpf factory at Pantin, France. That factory is known to have made paperweights, but a documented specimen is lacking. Until one is found, there is no evidence on which to base attributions.*

**292. France, factory unknown, ca. 1870-80**
Large pink rose and bud, the stem and leaves in two shades of green; opaque white ground.

D. 7.9 cm (3⅛ in.)
The Corning Museum of Glass (No. 58.3.206; gift of the Hon. Amory Houghton, Sr.)
Fluorescence: brilliant yellow-green
Color illustration, page 81

*See no. 291.*

**293. France, factory unknown, ca. 1870-80**
Large yellow rose and bud; green stem and leaves; brilliant blue ground.

D. 7.7 cm (3 in.)
The John Nelson Bergstrom Art Center and Museum, Neenah, Wisconsin (No. 252)
Fluorescence: brilliant yellow-green
Color illustration, page 81

*See no. 291.*

**294. France, factory unknown, ca. 1870-80**
Large, three-dimensional flower with white-lined blue petals and yellow center; ribbed green leaves; brilliant blue ground.

D. 8.0 cm (3⅛ in.)
The Art Institute of Chicago (gift of Arthur Rubloff, No. 37)
Fluorescence: brilliant yellow-green
Color illustration, page 79

*See no. 291.*

**295. France, factory unknown, ca. 1870-80**
Four purple cherries or plums on a twig, with green leaves in two colors; on an opaque white ground.

D. 7.5 cm (2¹⁵/₁₆ in.)
Private collection
Fluorescence: brilliant yellow-green
Color illustration, page 97

*See no. 291.*

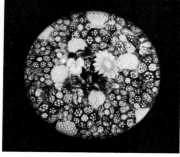

**296. France, factory unknown, ca. 1870-80**
Amber-colored pear on a branch with green leaves; vermilion ground.

D. 7.6 cm (3 in.)
The New-York Historical Society (No. 1965.402.C?; bequest of Mrs. Jennie H. Sinclair)
Fluorescence: brilliant yellow-green
Color illustration, page 98

*See no. 291.*

**297. France (?), Bohemia (?), factory unknown, ca. 1845-55**
Closely-packed clusters of star canes, with a floral plaque of enameled gold foil at the center.

D. 6.6 cm (2⅝ in.)
Private collection
Fluorescence: cloudy, light yellow
Color illustration, page 26

*The fluorescence of this weight is unlike that usually found in Baccarat, Clichy, and Saint-Louis weights. The bundling of canes into a dome of uneven height is unlike the smooth-topped domes one finds on close millefiori weights from these three factories. In addition, identical canes cannot be cited in signed weights. The attribution of this interesting piece is speculative.*

**298. France, factory unknown, late nineteenth century (?)**
Double spiral, yellow (straw-like) lattice basket, containing dark blue, light blue, pink, and white forget-me-nots; cut circular facets on the sides of the weight and one on the top.

D. 9.3 cm (3⅝ in.)
The Art Institute of Chicago (gift of Arthur Rubloff, No. 484)
Fluorescence: cloudy, light green (greener than Clichy)
Color illustration, page 85

*Although commonly attributed to Saint-Louis, this weight seems to have little in common (most obviously, its fluorescence) with other examples from that factory.*

**299. France, factory unknown, late nineteenth century**
Wild strawberry plant with two small red berries and yellow seeds, a large white flower and green leaves.

D. 7.8 cm (3 1/16 in.)
Private collection
Fluorescence: cloudy, lime-green
Color illustration, page 95

*The fluorescence is related to, but is visually different from that associated with Clichy.*

**300. France, factory unknown, ca. 1845-55**
Five red cherries on a forked, amber branch, with green foliage.

D. 8.0 cm (3⅛ in.)
The John Nelson Bergstrom Art Center and Museum, Neenah, Wisconsin (No. 295)
Fluorescence: cloudy, gray-green
Color illustration, page 97

*Formerly attributed to Baccarat, but its fluorescence is not consistent with other weights from that factory.*

**301. France, factory unknown, ca. 1845-55**
Encased circular sulphide plaque with molded, beaded edge, painted with a bouquet of naturalistic flowers; encircled with a ring of pink canes.

D. 7.5 cm (2 15/16 in.)
Private collection
Fluorescence: cloudy, yellow-green
Color illustration, page 118

**302. France, factory unknown, ca. 1811-50**
Sulphide disk, with decoration on both sides; the obverse with Napoleon Bonaparte holding the infant King of Rome over an elaborate font, inscribed "BAPTEME DU ROI DE ROME/M.DCCCXI" at the bottom, "LAFITTE DEL." on the base, and "ANDRIEU FECIT." at the side; the reverse with two rings of castellated buildings, each inscribed with the name of a city ("PARIS," "ROME," "AMSTERDAM," etc.), and inscribed "A L'EMPEREUR/LES BONNES VILLES/DE L'EMPIRE" in the center; the faces of the plaque domed, the edge decorated with cut spiral gadrooning.

D. 9.1 cm (3 9/16 in.); Thickness: 5.3 cm (2 1/16 in.)
Illinois State Museum, Springfield (No. 702316; gift of Morton D. Barker)
Fluorescence: cloudy, gray-green (not Clichy)
Color illustration, page 118

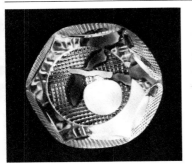

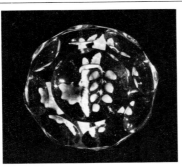

**303. France, factory unknown, ca. 1845-55**
Peach on a green branch, with three green leaves; six circular cut facets on the sides of the weight and one on the top, the bottom of the weight cut with small diamonds.

D. 5.4 cm (2⅛ in.)
Mr. and Mrs. Franklin Schuell, South Bend, Indiana
Fluorescence: cloudy, pale lavender
Color illustration, page 95

*The fluorescence is unlike "typical" Saint-Louis fluorescence, to which it has usually been attributed; similar to the fluorescence of the bunch-of-currants weight (no. 304).*

**304. France, factory unknown, ca. 1845-55**
A bunch of red currants on a green stem, suspended from a tendril-entwined amber branch, with green leaves; cut circular facets on the sides of the weight and one on top.

D. 5.0 cm (2 in.)
Mr. and Mrs. Franklin Schuell, South Bend, Indiana
Fluorescence: cloudy, pale lavender
Color illustration, page 97

*As noted previously (p. 94), the decorative details—stem, leaves and berries—are related to similar motifs in Saint-Louis weights, but the fluorescence is unlike "typical" Saint-Louis fluorescence, to which factory it has usually been attributed.*

**305. France, factory unknown, ca. 1870-80**
Strawberry on a curved stem, with several green leaves.

D. 6.8 cm (2¹¹/₁₆ in.)
Private collection
Fluorescence: cloudy, gray-blue
Color illustration, page 95

**306. France (?), factory unknown, ca. 1845-55**
Sulphide profile portrait of Lafayette, on a transparent deep blue ground.

D. 7.4 cm (2¹⁵/₁₆ in.)
The New-York Historical Society (No. 1965.412.B; bequest of Mrs. Jennie H. Sinclair)
Fluorescence: cloudy gray (not Baccarat)
Color illustration, page 116

**Arrowhead cane.** Cluster of canes with motifs of three lines coming together at a point, reminiscent of an arrowhead (also known as a "crowsfoot" cane).

**Aventurine.** Glass spangled with green or copper-colored flakes.

**Basket.** Funnel-shaped lattice support, usually holding fruit or flowers; the sheath of stripes on the sides and bases of Clichy weights; sometimes a realistic latticework basket with foot, rim, and handle.

**Carpet (or carpet ground).** A cushion of canes of one color or design.

**Close millefiori.** Sections of a variety of canes, packed closely and randomly together.

**Crown weight.** A hollow weight incorporating white or colored filigree rods arranged vertically on the sides and drawn together at the top.

**Filigree.** A rod incorporating thin white or colored spiral threads, giving the appearance of lace. See also *torsade*.

**Filigree ground.** Scattered, short lengths of filigree rods, forming a bed for other decoration; also called "muslin," "upset muslin," "gauze," or "lace" grounds.

**Garland.** Chains of millefiori canes, arranged in patterns of loops, circles, etc., often intertwined.

**Handcooler.** An ovoid, egg-shaped glass object, said to have been used to cool the palms of a lady's hands.

**Jasper.** A granular ground of particles of two or more colors.

**Marbrie.** A weight with colored loops, usually on a white background and encased; a term of unknown origin, perhaps derived from *marbre* suggesting marble or marbleized.

**Moss.** A cane with either green rods or green rods and white stars; often assembled in a carpet giving the appearance of a bed of moss. Also sometimes termed a "prairie ground."

**Mushroom.** Millefiori canes arranged to form an upright, circular, spreading stem and convex cap.

**Pedestal.** A weight on a spreading or basket-shaped support; also called a *piedouche* weight.

**Posy.** A small bouquet of flowers, usually formed of millefiori canes.

**Reground.** Reshaped by grinding and polishing to remove scratches and bruises.

**Sandy ground.** The ground on a few weights, most notably the salamander weights, with an appearance of large-grained sand, generally mixed with grains of opaque white and translucent green.

**Stardust ground.** A carpet of canes made up of clusters of tiny white stars.

*Torsade.* A circular filigree ring, incorporating white and/or colored spiral threads.

**Waffled.** Pincered, lattice decoration used on flower petals and leaves.

Bedford, John. *Paperweights*. New York: Walker and Co., 1968.

Bergstrom, Evangeline H. *Old Glass Paperweights, Their Art, Construction, and Distinguishing Features*. Chicago: Lakeside Press, 1940.

Bergstrom, John Nelson, Art Center and Museum, Neenah, Wisconsin. *Glass Paperweight Symposium Lectures*, June 25-28, 1967.

Bergstrom, John Nelson, Art Center and Museum, Neenah, Wisconsin. *Glass Paperweight Symposium Lectures*, June 27-30, 1976.

*Bulletin of the Paperweight Collectors' Association*. Ed. Paul Jokelson. P.O. Box 128, Scarsdale, New York. Annual, beginning 1954.

Cloak, Evelyn Campbell. *Glass Paperweights of the Bergstrom Art Center*. New York: Crown Publishers, Inc., 1969.

Elville, E.M. *Paperweights and Other Glass Curiosities*. London: Spring Books, 1954.

Gayle, Mary Redus. *Glass Paperweights from the Estelle Doheny Collection*. Ephrata, Pa.: Science Press 1971.

Hollister, Paul, Jr. *Glass Paperweights at Old Sturbridge Village; The J. Cheney Wells Collection*. Sturbridge, Mass.: Old Sturbridge Village, 1969.

Hollister, Paul, Jr. *The Encyclopedia of Glass Paperweights*. New York: Clarkson N. Potter, Inc., distributed by Crown Publishers, Inc., 1969.

Hollister, Paul. *Glass Paperweights of the New-York Historical Society*. New York: Clarkson N. Potter, Inc., distributed by Crown Publishers, Inc., 1974.

Hollister, Paul. *Glass Paperweights: An Old Craft Revived*. Coupar Angus, Scotland: William Culross & Sons, 1975.

Imbert, R. and Amic, Y. *French Crystal Paperweights*. Paris: Art and Industry, 1948. In French and English.

Jokelson, Paul. *Antique French Paperweights*. Scarsdale, New York: Paul Jokelson, 1955.

Jokelson, Paul. *One Hundred of the Most Important Paperweights*. Scarsdale, New York: Paul Jokelson, 1966.

Jokelson, Paul. *Sulphides: The Art of Cameo Incrustation*. New York: Thomas Nelson & Sons, 1968.

McCawley, Patricia K. *Antique Glass Paperweights from France*. London: Spink & Son Ltd., 1968.

McCawley, Patricia K. *Glass Paperweights*. London: Charles Letts, 1975.

Mackay, James. *Glass Paperweights*. New York: Viking Press, 1973.

Manheim, Frank J. *A Garland of Weights*. New York: Farrar, Straus and Giroux, 1967.

Mannoni, Edith. *Les Sulfures et boules presse-papiers*. Paris: C. Massin, 1974.

Melvin, Jean S. *American Glass Paperweights and Their Makers*. Rev. and enlarged ed. New York: Thomas Nelson, Inc., 1970

Selman, Lawrence. *Paperweights for Collectors*. Santa Cruz, Calif.: Paperweight Press, c.1975.